The Fluency of Light

sightline books

The Iowa Series in Literary Nonfiction

Patricia Hampl & Carl H. Klaus, series editors

Aisha Sabatini Sloan
The Fluency of Light

*Coming of Age in a
Theater of Black and White*

University of Iowa Press   Iowa City

University of Iowa Press, Iowa City 52242
Copyright © 2013 by Aisha Sabatini Sloan
www.uiowapress.org
Printed in the United States of America
Text design by Richard Hendel

The University of Iowa Press is a member of
Green Press Initiative and is committed to
preserving natural resources.

Printed on acid-free paper

ISBN-13: 978-1-60938-160-8
ISBN-10: 1-60938-160-2
LCCN: 2012945879

FOR MY PARENTS

Contents

Someone, a child for example . . . a neighbor another—
O how unfathomably remote they all appear.
—RAINER MARIA RILKE, "Sonnets to Orpheus"

The Fluency of Light

Los Angeles, California

Birth of the Cool

os Angeles glinted like an Austrian crystal through the windows of my mother's Toyota Corolla. "Why can't daddy and I be white like you?" I whined. We were on the freeway. Gray paths snaked their way toward the ocean. Green signs held a collection of numbers and letters, some of which indicated that we were almost home. My mother said, "I love your coloring. I wish I had skin the same color as you." The word *glint* comes from the Middle English *glent*, and it is of Scandinavian origin. My origin is Italian and Black—brown Afros on both sides.

At the time I had a boyfriend, and he was blonde. We had recently gotten married during a free period at our preschool, which was owned by an energetic Indian woman named Hapi. She called the school Happyland. Alec had lifted some sort of fabric from my forehead so that we could kiss. I was four and brown and curly. Something about this romance made me regret myself, my appearance. If he said something to make me feel that way, I have forgotten what it was.

Los Angeles glints because of the way sunlight illuminates the smog that hangs in the polluted air. Blonde hair also glints. Brown, curly hair, for the most part, absorbs things. Like tangles and curious fingers. What I didn't take into consideration during this brooding moment of self-hatred was that Alec's little sister was brown like me. Adopted perhaps. Los Angeles was like that—multicolored. I grew up in a wealthy Westside neighborhood and attended schools dreamt up by former hippies. The city's racial metaphor for me felt like a pot of soup with a nice chef's salad, something casual and light and accompanied by a glass of iced tea. But this didn't prevent me from getting upset about race.

Thelonious Sphere Monk was born in Rocky Mount, North Carolina, in what some people have called "1918, question mark." He would eventually study music at Juilliard, travel the world, and live on in history as a founder of bebop whose piano improvisation was a cold, crazed shiver of genius. His face appears on a pin I once bought from a jewelry case in southeastern Alaska. Outside, the tide brought coldness from the ice-blue glacier across Kachemak Bay onto a beach littered with driftwood. Which is to say, his influence has permeated the globe.

I imagine him as a five-year-old boy, standing on a porch of peeling blue paint, prophetic. He closes his eyes and sees images of his future flash before him: a glacier, a cactus, the Berlin Wall. Then he opens them and sees the green hot South. He looks down on his skin, forty-two years before the Civil Rights Act. The journey from this small boy's present to the life he would lead seems enormous and impossible.

My girlfriend recently described Monk's piano playing with her hands. "You know how he goes over it, and you know what he's *not* playing, but he doesn't give it to you?" Her hands move around and establish an invisible area, then trip over it. "And he goes over it, and around it, and you want it so bad . . . or you don't? And finally he gives it to you. Or he doesn't." It strikes me to think of this man, alive in the long, pale hands of a twenty-five-year-old. Her fingers pantomime his jazz in the dry Tucson morning, underneath chirping birds. Long, skinny branches with thin thorns make shadows on the patio floor.

My father's mother, Argusta, was born in Alabama. Her family lived next door to a white family, and all the children played together. The father of the neighboring family was a violent man when he drank, and his children would often run to my great-grandparents' house for safekeeping. They hid in the attic for hours. My great-grandmother made sure they were safe, then took out her Bible and waited downstairs for their father to arrive. "I know what you're going to say," he would moan, as she pushed him down and began to recite passages. Argusta and my great-aunt Cora May waited near the train tracks for their neighbors after school on cold winter days, so that they could all walk home together, as their parents had commanded.

One of the girls in the white family was nicknamed "Nig." Eventually, she grew up and got married. She came back home one day to show off her new husband, and bumped into my grandmother, who went into a fit of nostalgia. "Nig! How you been!" She screamed, and gave her old friend a huge hug. The husband went into a rage. He demanded that my grandmother get away from his wife, and how dare she address her that way? "What did you do?" I ask my grandmother on the phone. "I just laughed. I know it wasn't funny, but I couldn't help myself. He was making such a fuss."

My grandmother told me this story one recent afternoon. I was preparing to make dinner for company. "What chu makin'?" She asked. This is a question my mother asks me incessantly too, minus the southern twang. All of our conversations are often devoted to the preparation and consumption of meals. Every day my mother calls her mother-in-law in Detroit to chat on her way to work while slowly creeping along the 10 freeway toward downtown LA. "Your mamma made pork roast last night," my grandmother will inform me when we talk later on in the day. "I'd give anything for one of her salads."

The Internet includes footage of Thelonious Monk playing a concert in Berlin, in 1973. When you look at his face, he shows you nothing. His expression pretends to cover his interior life, but this is only a farce, because what's inside him comes spilling onto the piano keys, along with the sweat dripping off his hot, dark face. He wore a round, half-sphere-shaped hat, which often had a button on the top. He was known for his suits. Is it just my imagination, or do people tend to call well-dressed black men "dapper"? We'll call him that, but our eyebrows will be raised. His face and movements projected an air of mystery, as if to say, "There is more of me. You think you've got it, but you can't have it."

I have rented Clint Eastwood's documentary on the artist, *Thelonious Monk: Straight, No Chaser*. In one scene Monk stands in front of a door marked "Gentlemen." He begins to spin circles in place. Then he stops, takes a drag from his cigarette, and says, "I do that on the street. Somebody else do that, they'd put him in a straitjacket. Oh that Thelonious Monk, he's craaazy." Someone is laughing in the background. It is rare that Monk's mumbles clear the way for distinguishable words and phrases in the landscape of his language. Sometimes he would get up in the middle of a concert to spin in circles while somebody else was playing. It's possible that he was actually bipolar, but something about Monk's persona seems purposefully insolent.

Childish. And in a way, *black*. A woman I know once described a film director by saying, "He has the most bizarre outlook on life that I've encountered in a long time. He has such innocence, but it's such a black innocence, childishness about him." This idea seems relevant here. It is childish to spin around in a circle on stage when you are the featured performer of a concert, and it is bizarre, but in what way is it innocent?

My parents met in Detroit, in the public library where they both worked. My father called the circulation desk that my mother was manning and told her to look up to where he was standing several feet away. Their first date was to go to a friend's barbecue.

Several dates later, they were outside a restaurant for dinner. A man flashed a gun at them and said something about interracial couples. He and my father began an argument that eventually led them into the street. My father removed the gun from the man's possession, a tiny pistol. When my parents moved to Los Angeles in the 1970s, the two of them would go to the movies and wait for black women to tsk their tongues as they passed, calling my father a sellout with their narrowed eyelids and not looking my mother in the eye at all.

But I was rarely the target of overt racism during my childhood. There was the one time when, on a class trip to Catalina Island, a group of friends and I sat down with a kid from another school group. He lost a game of Go Fish and called me a nigger. "Why don't you go back to Africa with Martin Luther King?" he asked. Because my friends and I were smart enough to see the nonsense in his slander, and laughed about it, I was fine. I collected my playing cards from him, and my friends and I plotted to step on his toes at various points during the remainder of the boat ride.

What hurt about the experience was not his limp attempt at hatred, though. What bothered me was the loaded silence surrounding the issue. Three of my teachers, all of them white, sat in a booth within earshot of his tirade. I later told them what happened, and they said, "Yes, we heard. It seemed like you had everything under control." The fact that they hadn't said anything to me about it afterward made me feel strangely abandoned. Did they think this happened to me all the time? I had never been called that word before, and I wanted an adult to acknowledge its power and *then* dismiss it. Silence was a common way of handling the issue of race for most of the politically correct people I grew up around. But small questions would emerge like bright green pricks of grass out of the quiet. "Why is your mom white?" kids always, eventually, muttered—a sentence I always anticipated and always felt like a slap. There is no simple answer to this question, which is profoundly philosophical if you think about it.

When I was ten, a kid in my class did not like my curly hair, despite the fact that my mother had spent an hour combing, moussing, and decorating it with ribbon. It hung in shiny ringlets to my shoulders. He made a sour face and asked, "Why is your hair like that?" Every day for the next four years I wore it in a tight bun. Then I cut it off. Some might call me oversensitive.

During one period, later in my life, I listened to Billie Holiday sing "Solitude" over and over again, until her particular timing and the sweet croon of her inflection sewed the song onto my body. I can't pull on the melody without disturbing the sadness that it helped me survive. My first experience of heartbreak was nothing compared with what, of her life, Holiday was infusing into her music. In his essay "The Uses of the Blues," James Baldwin describes the time when someone asked Miles Davis why he was giving money to Holiday, when he knew she'd just spend it on heroin. Davis replied, "Baby, have you ever been sick?" The songs that Billie Holiday sings are draped in the biography of her own sadness, which is tugged on and burdened by the added sadness that her singing evokes in other people.

One of Monk's better-known compositions is called "Epistrophy," a play on the word *epistrophe*, which is pronounced the same way. Like anaphora, the repetition of the same word or words at the beginning of successive phrases, clauses, or sentences, epistrophe is a figure of speech meant to create emphasis by repetition of the same word or words at the end of successive phrases, clauses, or sentences. In one video recording of Thelonious Monk in Berlin, he plays the Ellington standard "Solitude," which immediately brings Holiday's voice to my mind. Toward the end of the song, he avoids playing the low note, which is supposed to punctuate the end of each line. This way, the most powerful part of this profoundly sad song is suspended in high notes. The pause of silence where a note should be feels like a comma, or an ellipsis, and he leaves us to fill in the blank. This way, the most emotionally conclusive moment of the line is left hanging, bringing to mind a singer too distraught to finish her sentences. If he were a singer, at this point in the song he would be saying:

I sit in my –	[chair]
I'm filled with de –	[spair]
There's no one could be so –	[sad]
With gloom every –	[where]
I sit and I –	[stare]
I know that I'll soon go –	[mad]

On that last line, instead of pausing or playing the note that evokes the word *mad*, he waits for the time of the word to pass, then shoves two discordant notes together, off to the side, capturing the pitch of crazy without leaving enough space for a word.

In *Thelonious Monk: Straight, No Chaser*, Monk's agent tells a story about the musician being interviewed by a reporter. The reporter asks, "What kind of music do you like?" and Monk replies, "I like all kinds of music." The reporter asks, "Do you like country music?" And Monk does not say anything. The reporter tries again. "Did you . . . do you like country music?" Monk looks at his agent and says, "I think the fella's hard of hearing."

I went to an elementary school with about five black kids, total, and I was one of three in my class. A girl named Erica, who lived in a wealthy, majority black neighborhood, was more of an acquaintance than a good friend, but we bonded. I spent a lot of energy making sure that everyone knew that just because I was one of two black girls, I was not necessarily interested in the only black boy in our class, a nice kid named Robert. Which is to say, I was a bit of a shit.

Despite this, I was not ignorant or disdainful of my own blackness. One day during PE class, Erica and I were across the playground from each other. As had happened on numerous occasions prior, our PE teacher, who was white, began calling my name to Erica, who pretended that she could not hear her until finally announcing, "I AM EH-REE-KA!" back. "That's it!" we told each other afterward. We arranged for an appointment with the principal, to discuss the dismissal of the already unpopular PE instructor, due to ignorance, bigotry, and discrimination. The principal humored us for half an hour, and we bragged to our parents about our political activities, but no one was fired.

One afternoon at Erica's house, I sat at the kitchen table while she sat on her father's lap. "You ever give your daddy sugar?" he asked me.

"No," I said.

"Why not?" he prodded. The moment pauses, clicks and glints in my memory.

"He's diabetic."

I sat confused as he and Erica spent the next two minutes laughing so hard they drooled. "What's so funny?" I asked. A glint is a spatially localized brightness. Her father caught his breath. "I don't mean *sugar*, I mean, do you ever give him love? Give him hugs and kisses?" I was black enough to get pissed off at my PE teacher, but not quite black enough to know how to talk right around *real* black people.

Thelonious Monk was born cool. After all, his *given* middle name is Sphere. But his childish, bizarre behavior is both black and *un*innocent because he participates in a larger tradition in which absurdity is a means of social protest. In other words, his innocence is feigned.

By spinning around in a circle onstage, he is escaping what must have been at that time a stultifying, deracinated social role — as a black man and a musician — with unpredictability. Rather than make an appointment with the principal in order to communicate "fuck you" to his PE teacher, he stands in silence at the sound of the wrong name as it is shouted across the playground. He dances in place, sings a song, does cartwheels — anything that is not what the woman is asking for. He lets the PE teacher yell her voice hoarse until she is able to realize her own mistake. If she walks away thinking that he is insolent, deaf, or an idiot, she is walking away believing a lie. And that lack of truth is what will hurt her, not him, in the greater scheme of things.

At another point in Eastwood's documentary, Monk walks into a recording studio. A short white record producer approaches him, sort of grabs at him in an attempt at greeting, and says, "Don't be jivin' me, man!" after which point he laughs hysterically. Monk is as still as a vase of flowers. The producer asks, "Where'd you get that hat?" and Monk replies,

"Oh yeah. That was given to me in Poland."

"Where?"

"Poland."

I cringe as I watch the producer dance around the room in a strained attempt to be similar to Monk, or to the other blacks or jazz musicians he's encountered. The result is, though unintentional, a near minstrel show of dissonance. But Monk's worldliness tucks itself into his own personal sphere of sophistication, into the inaudible soup of his speech, where the producer can't touch him. He chuckles underneath his breath. During some songs, he leaves a lit cigarette on the keys. When Monk plays "Solitude," the perspiration on his face reflects the light. To glint is to throw a brief glance at something, or to take a brief look. It also means to be shiny, as if wet. To glisten. To be looked upon by light.

Monk litters quiet moments throughout his music like a bread crumb path of crystals for us to follow. Where one might expect emphasis, he leaves us with silence, generating an exaggerated sense of loss. We fill in the missing beat, note, or word with a manifestation of our own longing. He makes the act of listening into an exchange or conversation. Like a church congregation, we say "chair," "despair," "sad," "where," "stare," and "mad," as if on cue, tripping off the edge of his melody, where he refuses to give us the comfort of an ending we anticipate. This is a form of communication that goes against the notion of communication altogether, a kind of induction of silence into language. By doing this, he suggests that we know *it*—we know this thing we are missing—already. We can put our hands around the space that it inhabits.

When I was in high school, I watched a lot of documentaries on cable television while making collages in my room. One day, *Thelonious Monk: Straight, No Chaser* came on. What I remember from that first time watching are the times when Monk was in the airport or on an airplane. At one point, he is sitting between a woman and his wife on a plane to London, and sunlight streams through the window. He is busy shuffling something, then he sits back, his eyes drift toward the camera, and he smiles, happy to be watched, perhaps aware of the audience beyond the cameraman. At that moment in his life, he was already starting to unravel. His son said, "He may pace for a few days, and then he'd get exhausted." And, "It's a startling thing to look your father in the eye and to realize he doesn't exactly know who you are." Only once did Monk mention anything about his own madness. In a cab in New York with his patroness and friend Baroness Pannonica de Koenigswarter, he said, "I think there's something wrong with me." When I listen to his music, I picture him pacing across the gate of an airport. A blue shadow loping across a screen of black and white.

I went to college in Minnesota, and my father came to visit one winter. We drove to a gas station just outside of St. Paul where you could pay after you pumped. "Can you imagine that in Detroit?" My dad asked. "Brothers be standing on the corner saying, 'They're giving gas away for free!'" My father saves black talk for only the funniest of jokes. I mostly hear it as he bellows on the phone with his best friend, Rodney, who still lives in Detroit. He will laugh so hard he'll fall out of the kitchen chair. I always wanted to tell him a joke that funny, and relished in these moments of uncontrolled joy. At that moment in Minnesota, I laughed until I spit. We were listening to "Ruby, My Dear" from a *Best of Thelonious Monk* album. The newly setting sun streaked the sky pink, and the horizon was blue and long. Pinpricks of snow reflected light in the soft landscape around us like scattered crystals. Brightness is defined as the location of a visual perception along the black-to-white continuum. Between blackness and whiteness, brightness holds clues about what connects one side to the other. "These niggers is crazy," my father said, when he finally caught his breath. "They givin' this shit away for free and they don't even know it." I put the track on repeat until we got to where we were going.

Detroit, Michigan

Fawlanionese

hen my dad was little, he worked. He helped his father to strip furnaces in the basements of the wealthy and gathered scraps of metal and coal off the streets to sell. But even though he learned to work doing physically exhausting, menial tasks, his expectations for himself had nothing to do with the expectations that the world had for black boys in 1950s Detroit. High school counselors prophesied his future with words like *plumber, electrician*, and *trade* and pursed their lips in amusement when he said that he'd like to go to college. They didn't know and probably wouldn't much care that this deeply creative child taught himself how to develop film in the bathroom at nine years old. He and his friend Rodney offered to do odd jobs shoveling snow and mowing lawns in a wealthy nearby neighborhood called Indian Village. One day, he turned to Rodney as they stood on the lawn of a historic white and brick home on Seminole street, and said, "One day I'm going to own a house here." And it didn't take too long before he did.

But his vision of the future soon began to push past the best that Detroit had to offer. He defied his guidance counselors by working seven times harder than anyone else, and graduated high school at age sixteen. After attending Wayne State University, he convinced CBS to allow him to be the network's first black cameraman. And then, in an unlikely burst of bizarre luck, the riots came. *Newsweek* magazine was desperate for photographs because their all-white staff of photojournalists feared braving the streets, so he got a job that may not have otherwise availed itself by simply walking the avenues near his own home with a camera. Not long after, he had a job waiting for him in Los Angeles. He hoped eventually to work in cities around the world.

Life happened alongside the hasty realization of his ambitions. He married young, had a daughter named Lisa, and got divorced. He worked as a manager at the public library, where he met my mom — an Italian girl who still lived with her parents near Eight Mile Road. The two of them decided to move to Los Angeles, and eventually they had me. My half sister remained in Detroit and became emotionally distant for a whole host of reasons that range in nature from obvious to profound.

We visit Detroit frequently to see family, but the house on Seminole has become a dream unrealized, a possible home that we decorated in our minds whenever the apartment we shared in Los Angeles seemed too small. As the years have passed, it has become a loaded notion, this house. It has been flooded and gnawed at by the dogs of neglectful renters, ransacked for its claw-foot bathtubs by thieves, and targeted by bigoted neighbors who complain about upkeep with only a thin smile covering their racism toward my father. These obstacles, like all the others he's faced, have made the house into an obsession. He cannot afford to refurbish the house in one fell swoop, but he tends to it slowly over time, like the soldier who keeps watch overnight while periodically stoking the fire. Whenever we go to Detroit for Christmas, the house must be wrestled and tamed in order to accommodate our basic needs for food, bathing, and warmth.

Far away from Detroit, in the middle of the nineteenth century, there was a man named Michael Faraday. When he was young he experienced obstacles similar to those my father faced. He was born to a blacksmith in South London, and he educated himself. A passion for chemistry grew out of the reading he did as an apprentice to a bookbinder and bookseller. His introduction to the world of science began when he approached a famous chemist at the Royal Institution in London with a book of rigorous notes and observations, and he eventually became the man's secretary. On his travels as an apprentice, he was forced to take the role of a servant, his body traveling and eating separately, though his mind was treated with admiration and respect. In order to push through to success, he had to convince the men and women around him of his basic human worth.

Long after he'd made a name for himself, he walked to the front of a lecture hall at the Royal Institution, surveyed the audience of students and said, "There is no better, there is no more open door by which you can enter into the study of natural philosophy than by considering the physical phenomena of a candle." I imagine him with tall, vertical wisps of bright white hair—backlit even when standing in a dark room. His smile would have been a small, blue glow, hovering above his body.

After picking me up from the Detroit airport, my dad tells me that he's been in pain all day. For hours, his foot felt cramped and numb, which for a diabetic can be cause to fear the worst—circulation problems sometimes require amputation. My face remains impassive during the silence that awaits his self-diagnosis. "I was at Home Depot when I decided to take off my shoe. I couldn't take it anymore. And do you know what? There was an extra sock in there, stuffed into the toe." We smile even though the punch line feels dark, and the air hears two tones of tired chuckles. We are here visiting family for Christmas. When we speak to my mother on the phone she, still in LA, tells us she is lonely and shopping for flannels. She'll join us in a week.

The car moves smoothly along an empty highway, exits on Van Dyke, and turns onto Seminole. We pass through a section of Detroit that is like an abandoned movie set—an artificial stage crumbling like burned wood after a fire. I find relief in the opulence of our historic home.

At dinner I can't help myself. I say, "It's a little pink." I am looking at the chicken in the soup that my dad made. On the plane ride over I entertained daydreams about eating a meal at Greektown—flaming saganaki cheese, olly salad, and chicken lemon soup. My father rarely cooked when I was growing up, and this is what I say to myself by way of explanation as I examine the meat in the chicken broth, the bloated neatness of the canned vegetables. My stomach reacts uneasily to the funny taste of the soup, which most likely has something to do with the fact that my dad used the hot spout of a water cooler and a Clorox wet wipe to clean my dish before putting the food inside. At the moment, there is no running water.

When it is time to go to bed, I change into a giant red nightgown that my dad laid out for me, and thick socks. As I join the teddy bear on the mattress, the bed makes a crunching sound and tips to the side, creating an anxiety that if I move too much I might cause the entire thing to fall over. The room was decorated with a child in mind, painted pink and situated close to the upstairs heating vent. But since the ideal of the room has been brought to life so slowly, over the course of so many years, the child has grown up, and the pinkness and stuffed animal have become palpable symbols for the gap between our family's dream and our reality. A photograph that I took when traveling with my father is framed and hanging over my maternal grandmother's blue-green armoire.

My father is across the hall. Before he calls goodnight to me, he says, "Pee pee," as in, "Use *this* bathroom if you have to." He doesn't normally say things like this to me, and it makes me feel momentarily stunned that I ever grew up and left home.

In the morning, my dad shaves in front of the mirror in the downstairs hallway. I take his picture with the digital camera that my parents gave me a few Christmases ago. Taking pictures and writing are crafts that my father and I share. He teaches me about f-stops, and I edit the beautiful essays and articles that he writes.

Because we have a long day of errands ahead of us, I have convinced him that we should drive to Starbucks. Coffee shops have become the space we carve out for bonding during holiday visits ever since I left. We often bring books and notepads with us on these trips, in case we need to discuss quotes and ideas with each other. Before we go in, as we walk across the small parking lot outside the café, I tell him to stand still while I take another picture of him in front of a brick wall with graffiti on it. This is a quiet way of acknowledging the expeditions we used to take together to shoot snapshots of graffiti during one of the summers we spent in Paris.

As we drink our coffee, and drive to make a stop at the Department of Water and Power, we talk about a book that he is reading—a dark parable about a father and his young son, struggling in a postapocalyptic world. My dad goes off to woo the woman in charge of turning our water back on in a beige cubicle across the room; I read the first pages of the book. The setting seems eerily similar to the streets of the cold, tired city outside. Sewers in a Detroit winter are always leaking warm columns of smoke into the bleached white air. Back in the car, I take a photograph of the mist as it rises outside the windshield, juxtaposed with a red traffic light, behind a stream of water that looks like a crack in the window. My dad sees the image as it flashes on the camera's LCD screen and says, "Damn. I wish I'd taken that."

A photograph of Faraday in his later years shows that he had bright white hair, but instead of wisping upward, the flame drapes down from a center part, curling at his ears. He based much of his career on making connections: between magnetism and electricity, magnetism and light. He also helped to build lighthouses, and acted as a judge for art exhibits. He strode through the Crystal Palace for the 1851 World's Fair, the sunlight catching on his hair as he passed by daguerreotypes, different types of security locks, and a prototype fax machine.

During his lectures, Faraday spoke as though he were a preacher, making sweeping parables: "Now the greatest mistakes and faults with regard to candles, as in many other things, often bring with them instruction which we should not receive if they had not occurred. We come here to be philosophers, and I hope you will always remember that whenever a result happens, especially if it be new, you should say, 'What is the cause? Why does it occur?' and you will, in the course of time, find out the reason."

When my sister had Jeremy and later LaShawn, it seemed like a new start for my father. He could be to his grandchildren what he'd never managed to be to his first-born child. And the relationship he built with Jeremy has been tender, and instructive. Jeremy has always been sweet and soft-spoken. One Christmas, when I was sixteen and Jeremy fourteen, he walked into the house on Seminole and crept slowly across the room. He moved like a deer, and I felt a surge of love and loss for him glowing in my chest. A flash of recognition, a mirror in his face, made me feel that this emotion was mutual. I felt this way again when I saw him at my grandfather's funeral. We've spoken very little to each other over the course of our lives. Now, at twenty-four, he is spending the second of many years to come in a Pennsylvania prison. When Faraday says that he will explain the candle, it seems he is trying to accomplish something that cannot be done. Like grief, like loss, like chaos, a concept so unrestrained as fire seems like it can and should not be contained by something so succinct as a "reason."

At night we go to buy Christmas presents at a mall in our rental car. A wealthy suburb of the festively lit city washes past the window in the form of a dark brown smear. My dad recalls the time that he fell down and lost consciousness three years ago, while fixing up the house. He underwent a CAT scan. A childhood friend named Buddy took him to the emergency room. And here's what's weird: he woke up in the same hospital his father had died in. On the one-year anniversary of his father's death. A specialist walked in and said, "What's wrong with you?" My father said he didn't know. I may as well mention that he is vehemently superstitious.

"Well, you don't have a brain tumor."

"Good."

"How much do you sleep?"

"Three or four hours a night."

"Why don't you go home and go to bed?"

Buddy had a round face as sweet as Jiminy Cricket's, and he passed away one week before my visit. My strongest memory of Buddy is from my grandfather's wake. We stood at the back of the room and he told me about eating well to stay healthy. "Lots of vegetables. Broccoli—steamed, not fried." Across the room, my grandfather looked like a figure made from purple wax in the coffin, so thin I couldn't see any semblance of him in his face. My father's grief at the time made it hard to look him straight in the eye.

On that day my father blacked out, on that morbid anniversary, he fell down from exhaustion, but maybe too at the specter of his father's death. Or at the specter of his own. I feel uneasy about this after we have arrived at the mall. I slam the door to the car and climb over a pile of snow that has collected on the curb.

"A combustible thing like that, burning away gradually, never being intruded upon by the flame, is a very beautiful sight, especially when you come to learn what a vigorous thing flame is—what power it has of destroying the wax itself when it gets hold of it, and of disturbing its proper form if it come only too near." The thing that helps to create the flame is itself destroyed. This is a perfect aphorism for my father's relationship to the house, or more specifically, for what it makes him do.

After hearing my paraphrase of Faraday's quote—"of disturbing its proper form if it comes only too near," my dad says, "It's kind of like a metaphor for life. Who was it, Einstein, that believed that energy couldn't be destroyed? Didn't he believe in reincarnation? Something about how energy goes back to itself, goes back to something larger than itself. It changes form. That's not like a candle, though. Is the wax ever really extinguished in a candle?" I say yes, it is, but perhaps I'm missing his point.

My first, clear memory of my grandfather is outside of the Indian Village house. I was probably around nine. The sidewalk outside was icy and he and my grandmother emerged slowly from a beige Cadillac. He was a big man, and tall, and did not really seem to see me. Everyone was afraid of slipping on the ice. When a candle is lit, sometimes it is in honor of someone who has died. As though their spirit, which still exists somewhere, is being maintained in the form of a flame.

I wake up in the middle of the night so hot I feel like I am being roasted at the marrow. I take off some of my layers—a portion of the flannel and wool and long underwear and knit hat that are covering me. Last night my dad woke up just as I got to the point where I could sleep. I could hear him downstairs and kept shouting at him to go to bed. "Can't!" he said. It's startling how easily I can hear him. There is no need to shout.

This morning there is a sound like a giant rat or ghost Pekingese running in the heat duct or upstairs. I hope it's my grandmother's wiener dog, Duke. When I get up to search around, the sound stops. Someone is downstairs talking to my dad—perhaps to turn the water on.

Later in the day, I find that it is my sister's friend Randy who has come to fix the pipes. He's about sixty, a giant with white hair and brown skin as light as milky coffee. His words, though in English, sound like another language blown through parched lungs. My father is excited about the repair. I ask to use the downstairs bathroom and my dad says, "Lemme fix it" and walks away to get a bucket of water to pour down the toilet bowl.

My dad walks into the kitchen and arranges an owl-shaped ceramic figure on the microwave.

"You know how long I've had this?"

"How long?"

"It's as old as I am. My father got it when I was a baby."

"A cookie jar?"

"*My* cookie jar."

He slips into loose-tongued blackness when he talks to Randy. He says, "Hey, man, you want your coat?"

I am disarmed by the way that my father reveres his cookie jar. The key word in his story is, of course, *father*.

Our attraction to flame seems to rest on the fact that it is an object without true form. A mythology of a thing, resembling an object but beyond substance. Then there is the fact that it has the power to give and take away life. Faraday says, "You have the glittering beauty of gold and silver, and the still higher lustre of jewels like the ruby and diamond; but none of these rival the brilliancy and beauty of flame. What diamond can shine like flame?"

My dad says, "Some smelly candles have chemicals in them that are harmful, which sort of defeats the purpose. Something that gives you light is giving you cancer at the same time . . . it reminds me of those buses. They made it so that the gasoline was scented, so that the exhaust wasn't so unpleasant. The buses had signs that said, 'Smell our smoke!' People would drive around, trying to smell the gas, thinking it was harmless. But it was still exhaust. It was like an invitation to suicide."

Not unlike a crazed motorist sniffing with his window down, my father's attraction to the house seems pathological. But I try to think about what being at the house means, and come upon a simple idea: *to work*. And I ask my dad, "What did grandpa have to say about work?"

"He respected work. That's how he determined a person's worth. And he was, grandpa was really very strong. People were taken with his strength. I remember we were tearing out this boiler. This man came in and said, 'Look at the muscles on this guy!' And he touched his muscles. And I was incensed. 'Why do you do this? Why do you let them do that?' And he said, 'So you won't have to. So you can go to school, and do what you want.' And I remember feeling ashamed and proud. Ashamed of myself and proud of him for doing what he did. When I was ten years old, working on this truck with him, we used to have to carry these humongous pieces of metal out to the truck. Coming out of the basement he would always tell me, 'Carry the front, guide it, and I'll push it to you.' But really he carried the bulk of the weight. He made me feel I was carrying my part of the weight, when really he was holding it off of me."

It will be three months before my father leaves Detroit, even though it was only supposed to be a three-week visit. He'll push his plane ticket back every week. He'll say, "The electricity went out again," or he'll tell me how cold it is on the third night without a furnace. He will camp out like an old man in a graveyard. Faraday offers, "I have seen boys about the streets, who are very anxious to appear like men, take a piece of cane, and light it, and smoke it, as an imitation of a cigar."

Cora May just moved to Detroit to live with my grandmother. The street, Baldwin, where they live, where my father grew up, looks like the stereotype of run-down Detroit: a black urban neighborhood. The sun sets pink over an empty, snow-covered lot with pieces of wood and metal piercing through the white. A young woman limps as she walks down the sidewalk, her eyes glazed. People stop by all the time to sell my grandmother "junk," as my dad calls it, and sometimes my grandmother plays along.

But her sister, Cora May, is not about to play along with anyone. She wants to buy a gun with my dad before he leaves town. She tells us that just before we came, a girl stopped by the house for a quarter. The girl came inside, wandered into the kitchen, and chatted with them in the living room. "She had a can of peaches too, she'd took from my sister's cupboard. I didn't say anything. Them niggers don't like me. They don't stop by as much since I live here."

Her voice is both gruff and honeyed. Her hair is dyed red on top of the white. Some nights, she drinks from a forty-ounce bottle of Coors Light in the evening while she and her sister watch the evening news.

There is a silence in the conversation. I look at my grandmother, half blind in a brown armchair. She used to wear wigs, but now she lets her thinning white hair breathe, collects it in a small braid at the base of her head. She and I have been talking on the phone over the years since my grandfather died. We discuss meals, the weather, and our pets. When she first met my grandfather, she was convinced that it was Cora he was after. The two of them are quite competitive. I can't talk for too long to one sister without acknowledging the other.

But Cora May has a lot to say. She reminisces about going to work at the hospital after the riots broke out when Martin Luther King Jr. was killed. "Our people ain't right," she says. Once, a woman who wanted her job as the main cafeteria cook threatened to beat her up.

Cora May just laughed. She told the people she worked with, "Let her try. Y'all 'll be eating nigger stew for breakfast."

When my grandmother was still deep in mourning after my grandfather's death, she'd tell me about how the two of them would spend winter days in the kitchen, near the oven, telling stories.

Daughter: "Do you have any memories about candles? Candles and your mother?"

Father: "Only running around her house with them, trying not to set any of those boxes she has around on fire. I went out and bought her some battery-powered lights so she wouldn't have to set anything on fire in case the power went out again."

Daughter: "Do you have any memories about candles and your father?"

Father: "No. Seems to me the power never went out when my father was around."

Daughter: "What about fire? Memories of your father and fire?"

Father: "[pause] Yes. Driving down the Ford Freeway with flames coming from the hood of the car. Because to start the car he had to pour ether in. And when ether got hot it started a fire. We drove in the direction of Chicago, trying to put the fire out by going faster. None of the locks on the truck worked, so if we crashed we would have died for sure. There was a rope tied from his door to my door. . . . And he had control of the knot. It was something out of Greek mythology. This flaming stead, this flaming horse, driving down the highway. We tried to put it out by going faster."

Faraday: "If I take a flame sufficiently large, it does not keep that homogeneous, that uniform condition of shape, but it breaks out with a power of life which is quite wonderful."

Neither Randy nor my father accept when I offer to pour them cups of coffee. Randy and his round belly pass by me in the hallway to go downstairs. My father follows, stepping gingerly down the steep stairs into the basement. He is having fun.

With hazelnut creamer, the coffee is sweet and the pot seems endless. I am engrossed by the book I am reading in the kitchen, *The Professor's Daughter*, by Emily Raboteau — perhaps because its characters somewhat resemble my own family. It takes a moment for me to notice when water starts to rain from the ceiling. I glance at the liquid seam shimmying down the wall and decide to finish my paragraph before getting a bucket to catch the leak. When I do, I see that it's raining in the living room too. As the house becomes enlivened by disaster, Randy's voice comes shouting up from the basement: "It's not . . . comin' from de baaathroom. We got to find deese pipe." He is from Bali, but for some reason that I can't fathom, he likes it better in Detroit. A Balinese accent, at least to me, is not unlike a Jamaican one, and it comes as a total incongruity in the cold, dirty adventure that is the house.

A little while later, my uncle Ted knocks on the front door. I don't have vivid memories of my dad's sister, Mavis, or her husband Ted until a few years ago, after my grandfather's funeral. I remember, despite the difficulty of the occasion, that I could feel love soften the strangeness, an easy kindness and affection that came quietly and was everywhere. Randy and my father are peering upward at the ceiling in the living room, dodging and not quite dodging threads of the leak. I let my uncle in and give him a hug. "Ohh," he says when he sees the mess. He explains that he is on his way over to my grandmother's house, where an electrical box is sizzling. He tells my dad, "I was going to ask if your mother and aunt could stay here, but it looks like maybe that's not . . ." My dad is standing with his hands on his hips. He interrupts Ted's train of thought. "What do you mean, a box is sizzling?"

I listen to them for a while, sitting on the stairwell. Then I hear a sound. I say,

Dad?

"Yes sweetheart."

"What's that sound?"

"Water."

"I realize that. Where is it coming from?"

"The living room."

"*I realize that.* Where else?"

"Upstairs."

"Where upstairs?"

"Oh. Your room."

I had felt perfectly calm while the force of a thousand seas pushed in through the cracks of the house. Now, I am upstairs shouting.

"Couldn't you have told me this a half hour ago?" My body is alive with anger. The yellow streams of water leaking directly into my bed and suitcase smell exactly how they look. I squeeze water out of fabric and throw the blankets off my bed over the banister.

Ted leaves quietly. Randy turns the water off and we prepare to drive him home. I think about how my father said, "I'm happy with the little things, like water and heat" a few minutes before the house began to rain. But these things are not "little" as far as I'm concerned. From where I'm sitting, it looks like he's trying to move the universe around as though it were a piece of furniture. After we've battled fire and water, I'm sure that wind and earth will present themselves as obstacles if we want to make this house livable before Christmas.

I've always felt confused at the fact that my sister was as distant as she was. But looking back, it seems that the forces that keep us apart and bring us together are about as inevitable as gravity. Faraday says, "For the same force of gravity which holds worlds together holds this fluid in a horizontal position, and if the cup be not horizontal, of course the fluid will run away in guttering." The same force of gravity which holds worlds together. It is both obvious and startling to realize that the same thing that keeps worlds together is at work in the operations of a candle.

My dad is locking the door to the house with arthritic fingers while Randy and I wait in the car. Randy says, "Last year they told me I had a bleeding ulcer. Doctor gave me a day." There are tiny braids in his long, white beard. "That was one year ago tomorrow. I stopped drinking alcohol and started to drink three gallons of water per day. I take herbs." He returns to the doctor tomorrow.

"I guess he used to be your sister's boyfriend," my father tells me when Randy begins to cross the street, away from our car and toward his home. My sister is about twenty years younger than Randy, and two hundred pounds lighter. Her skin is three times as dark. And she didn't spend more than a few months living under the same roof as our father when she was growing up. This is a difficult fact to let go of as I look at Randy, now taking the steps slowly, an old, sick, sweet man in his light gray sweat suit.

Both men have served a strangely similar role in my sister's life.

Both men have used the phrase "one year and one day" to begin a story to me in this rental car. Both stories have been about not dying.

After dropping Randy off, we have a dinner of perfect fried chicken at my grandmother's house. These are some of the phrases that I hear:

375 Magnum
Straight razor
Lye in a fruit jar
Machete

All of these words come out of my great aunt Cora May's mouth, in a nostalgic tone. "I used to have," "I know how to use," "I used to carry,"

Cora May chews tobacco and tells more stories about her life in New Jersey. This time it's about stepping over harmless winos, and dodging bleary-eyed dope addicts. At some point someone says "Don't give away my sugar!" and what they mean is, "affection."

Back at the house, I open a bottle of old champagne and attempt to drink the entire thing. I use rubber cement to glue magazine pictures onto cards for Christmas. I watch late-night TV until my dad turns off the oven. This inadvertently causes the TV screen to flash and go blank.

At 1:18 A.M., I say, "Good night, Dad."

"Don't go to bed—Oh. You're . . ." I am rubbing lotion into my hands. "I wanna load this stuff into a bag." I hold a big, plastic garbage bag open as he sweeps plaster into it. These are remnants of the ceiling that fell during the leak. He explains that if we do this, when we wake up, it won't look so bad. He says, "I think this house is testing me."

"When wasn't it testing you?"

"It's testing me to see how dedicated I am to it." When I wake up the kitchen is spotless.

Not many of my father's journalist friends are from Detroit, but one lives not far from my grandmother. He takes long walks along the river from his house, wearing several layers of coats in the wintertime to work up a sweat. We've invited him over for Christmas, because he is far away from his own family. One month after Christmas he will be attacked, during one of his long walks, or maybe on the way to the dry cleaner; stabbed in the back with a razor. All the bones in his face will be broken. He will try to walk out of the hospital with a broken body, for lack of insurance, and fail. The nurses will quiz all his visitors, in case one is the man who'd like to finish the job. Faraday says, "The air flows in so irregularly that you have what would otherwise be a single image broken up into a variety of forms, and each of these little tongues has an independent existence of its own. Indeed, I might say, you have here a multitude of independent candles." Perhaps a candle, which can come to be many candles in one, will never represent just one thing. Which is to say, it's not only my grandfather who is honored through this incessant upkeep of the house but something larger that is perpetuated, some other notion of clarity or cohesion.

My mom arrives. The disasters of the house seem less tragic when she's around. Nonetheless, we all have a fight in the middle of the grocery store, in the wine aisle. My mother comes from a culture that shouts as a means of everyday communication, and the tradition has lived on in her small brood. Loudness does not mean the same thing that it does in other households, nor does it mean that we don't laugh equally as hard soon after an argument. But no one in the store is aware of this as we take turns being the victim. I storm off to cry and get samples of gourmet coffee, peering in the faces of other customers in search of some shared inner torment. We buy two tons of food, return to the house, and begin to cook. Eventually it is Christmas Eve.

We plan to pick up my grandmother and great aunt at seven so that they can sleep over and wake up in the house on Christmas. For the moment, we relax, munch on snacks, and chat over the television. At five o'clock, my father's phone rings. From his tone, I know that it is my sister. "Couldn't you have mentioned this sooner?" My niece is singing at a Christmas mass in an hour.

Here is a list of observations that I wrote in my journal about the night: My father wears bright red ski overalls and a knit cap, and he carries a TV-news-sized camcorder. Lashawn, my niece, speaks her part softly, embarrassed and eyeing her grandfather's camera. My mother and I fall asleep once the mass starts, and my sister hands us peppermints wrapped in cellophane when we wake up. When the man gets up to the pulpit to sing "O Holy Night," my sister says quite loudly, "I love this song. I hope he doesn't mess it up." And he doesn't. And I hear, for the first time, that the first lyric of the chorus is not, as I'd always thought, some other language, something like "Fawlanionese." It is "Fall on your knees," and for a second this fact makes the world go white and slowly come back into focus. I listen to the verse that follows as though for the first time, "Hear the angel voices." I correct myself when I turn to my sister and say "my father" instead of "ours." And she calls out "Daddy" when she wants to tell him something. And she makes us laugh or roll our eyes about every other thing. She reaches out to the homeless man in the pew in front to grab his hand, and brings it together with my father's hand to hold, so the man won't be without company during the liturgy of the Eucharist.

At the end they ask us to buy candles and have them blessed. Lisa buys one for me, my mother, our father, her daughter, and herself. We all have the silent, painful awareness that my nephew Jeremy is not there. We take the candles up to the altar, to the African priest with an accent that Lisa giggled about a few minutes before. We go up as a family, and have our candles blessed. The fact that we are, at this moment, a family — the fact that this is what separates our group from the others — feels singular. It is a moment that other people in the church wouldn't know to notice, and the quiet normalcy of our being together feels, more than the Christmas holiday, like a pretty good reason to celebrate. So we consecrate with a candle. "You can keep this one, but we're going to take the rest home with us," my sister tells the priest. And she says, "This way we can each have one in our houses."

When we reach the door of the church, she says, "Careful out there. This is Michigan. People are crazy. Our church has a security van."

The unexpected charm of our evening puts us all in a perfect state of reverence for the present. But we are standing on something fragile. The last hour of peacefulness has come after days of anger, frustration, and fatigue. On the way home I break the mood. My dad asks if he can make a quick stop at the store and I say, "I have a lot of gifts to wrap," which sets off a kind of electric silence. He turns onto Seminole and parks, walks up to the house, and opens the door. I ask him to open up, to tell me how he feels. "I can take it!" he says, "I'm fine," which only makes me angrier. So I pester, I try to get my mom involved. I stand on the stairs and my mom stands near the banister as he moves things from one room to another. I push and I push, and finally, we break. There is a fight loud and cathartic as a spray of sparks.

My father says, "Last night, I asked you to plug in a lamp, and you said you couldn't. Because you had just washed your hands. So instead, you watched your father crawl on the floor and do it himself." I'd been waiting for that. It felt right to be scolded for a moment of such overt selfishness. I couldn't say much in my defense, even though during the moment in question, I was acting out of what felt to be a hard-earned vengeance.

And he said, "My mother's house nearly caught on fire, and your uncle stops here first, to see if we can take her. But as of now, there's no way for her to take a shower. And on top of that, everybody is mad at me. I just want this place to be hospitable for *one night*." We scream and complain, apologize just as loudly, and eventually we are laughing, grateful to be on each other's side. His stoicism comes undone just enough for us to collectively accept and unburden him of some small pieces of his stress.

The next few hours are spent moving mattresses up and downstairs, from bed to bed, scraping our arms on creaky bed frames and getting spiderwebs from the dark, dusty corners of the master bedroom caught like cotton candy in our mouths. The master bedroom is currently being used for storage, but one day my dad plans to transform it into an exhibition room. He'll hang art on the walls and install a projection screen for film viewing. Maybe the house can be a kind of artist's residence? We start to brainstorm on this plan. It can't be too tough to strike up a connection with the art school downtown, right? Meanwhile, a large, framed poster of Miles Davis leans in wait against the wall.

"Now the greatest mistakes and faults with regard to candles, as in many other things, often bring with them instruction which we should not receive if they had not occurred. We come here to be philosophers, and I hope you will always remember that whenever a result happens, especially if it be new, you should say, 'What is the cause? Why does it occur?' and you will, in the course of time, find out the reason." And when you realize that there is no cause, the cause is simply life itself, you light a candle, or work to save a house from falling on its knees. And as you stand there, a clown with your arms and legs akimbo, just barely keeping the walls upright, you think about all the people you'd like to keep safe with the warmth of a flame, and within the fragile walls of that house. But what will happen if you let go?

Northfield, Minnesota

Fade to White . . . .

I. Topography

The Mobil travel guide I've checked out from the library says that Minnesota is home to "craggy cliffs" and "native prairie land where buffalo still roam." The man who founded the city of Luvurne called it "the Garden of Eden." There is a place known as "Blue Earth" where the ground is made of blue-black clay. I remember my freshman year of college, hanging back from the group during geology field trips so I could feel the long stretch of space exist quietly around me. I found the expanse of Minnesota at times so still that I had to listen for it, wait it out, as though it were holding its breath. I was looking down when the teacher told us, "all of this was once an ocean."

II. Rites of Passage

When I was young, the only holocaust I'd heard of was stranded in a distant past. I didn't realize that people were fleeing acts of perverse violence even then. This seems a common trick among the privileged: we teach our children about hatred as though it were a faraway land. But one day we have to break the news: that it never stopped. It never will. And what of that distant land—is that here? One thing is for sure: the refugees are coming.

According to a 1946 edition of *Negro Digest*, experts were saying that every year between 15,000 and 30,000 Americans once classified as black had "gone over" to the white side. Others thought the number of blacks who left the black community in order to pass for white annually was more like 200,000. They describe this movement as an "annual migration." For example: after being called a "Nigger Lover" and told to leave the black section of a baseball game, one light-skinned African American man moved to the Midwest, married a white woman, and hoped his history would not reveal itself in the pigment of his children.

My anthropology professor put in a video in which teenaged males in an African tribe were asked to lie down and hold still. Blades were used to slice a series of incisions, called *gaar*, across their foreheads. Tears and blood pooled from their heads during the initiation, but many of these young men remained admirably motionless. It startled our professor, he told us, when one day he was at the local grocery store and he saw a tall, thin man with dark skin and *gaar* on his head. It must have seemed as if the man had stepped off the screen of the documentary and into a midwestern landscape. I imagine the man to have been wearing a white and blue windbreaker, the cold winter sun glaring behind.

Significant numbers of people have moved from the Horn of Africa to the Midwest since the 1970s. Minneapolis and St. Paul have some of the largest communities of Somalis, Ethiopians, and immigrants from the Sudan in the United States.

In a book about the Somali diaspora entitled *Yesterday, Tomorrow*, one man explains to his son how he came to leave Somalia: "Let me tell you that we fled because we met the beasts in us, face to face."

III. Aviation

According to the book *Nuer Journeys, Nuer Lives*, some of the women and men traveling from the horn of Africa to Minnesota feared that the plane, or "sky boat," would fall. They found the flight "nearly impossible to endure."

IV. Bankruptcy/Insolvency

The *Negro Digest* article notes that an investigator from the Midwest calculated, based on census data, that "in the two decades from 1890 to 1910 the Negro race in this country lost approximately 600,000 persons."

V. Bodies of Water

During the first week I spent in Minnesota, we set out in canoes to float the jagged seam that separates Minnesota from Ontario. Because many routes had dried up over the summer, we waded for what felt like forever, carrying the canoes overhead in portage. The rocks were slippery and some much deeper than others. I remember the sound my shin made against rock when I fell, like a pop, even though there's no way I could have heard it. For about ten minutes we stood still in the water, making jokes about the stories they'd tell of our disappearance.

In *Negro Digest*, "passing" is described as "crossing over, crossing the line or going over to the other side."

VI. Discourse

When one Nuer man arrived at the airport in Minnesota, he said, "What is that?" Outside, it was "white, white everywhere." He wasn't sure what had happened to the trees. Another man picked up the white substance and said, "That's called snow."

VII. Articulation

In an English-Amharic dictionary, the first exercise for learners to translate reads like a mystery unfolding. One wonders what the author's life must have been like in order for him to believe that these sentences would be useful:

1. Come. 2. Be quiet (pl.) 3. Wait here. 4. Look (pl.)! 5. Call Ahmed. 6. Go there. 7. Is it peace? It is peace. 8. Hi! Bring it here. 9. Bring a cup. 10. Untie the man. 11. Take away the table. 12. Now fasten the straps. 13. Look at the rain. 14. Follow (pl.)

the river. 15. Put a fire in. 16. Bring (some) other clothes. 17. Hi!
Come here: bring another strap. 18. Put the clothes on the table.
19. Put the eggs on the fire. 20. Go (pl.) now: goodbye. 21. Call
the cook now. 22. Light another fire. 23. Put (pl.) the table there.
24. Now call the men. 25. Put the clothes on the tree.

In the Ethiopian language book, there is an exercise in which an
unusual verb is introduced: *addee*. "To whiten." For example, on page
seventeen it says, "Whiten the walls. Call the boy."

VIII. Transport

Negro Digest goes on to say that if a black man decided to pass
for white, he could claim to be any number of European nationali-
ties. "Sometimes he prepares for the adventure by learning Spanish,
French, Italian or Portuguese, or by cultivating an accent." But what
other attitudes must be taken? Words only constitute a small part of
communication.

IX. Lowest Temperature

In the book *The Winter Sun*, Fanny Howe describes the sun as having "an intention infusing it, a presence that had no attributes, not
even love."

When assigned to do a self-portrait for my photography class se-
nior year, I set out through the main streets of the small town on
cold days with black-and-white film. On a Sunday when no one was
around, I put the camera on timer, and crouched down by a pile of
tires outside of a closed auto mechanic's shop. I took off my jacket,
scarf, shirt, and bra, and leaned in close to the bumper of a pickup
truck, waiting for the shutter release to click.

X. Citizenship

When James Baldwin sat down to talk with anthropologist Margaret Mead, he told her: "By teaching a black child that he is worthless,

that he can never contribute anything to civilization, you're teaching him how to hate his mother, his father and his brothers."

When some Nuer were interviewed in refugee camps, they quickly realized that the plots they'd recalled were in need of revision. If, for example, Gatluak Luoth wanted to qualify as a refugee, he could not simply recount conditions in which warfare and famine were prevalent. He had to pinpoint a more acute aggressor, as if reprocessing his story for the whim of a film noir director: "I told them that the soldiers killed my father and then my mother and then they were looking for me." Another man failed the exam when he told the interviewer that he was seeking medical assistance for his sick child. He said, "It's funny that when you tell them the truth, they can't accept you."

Margaret Mead told James Baldwin, "We'll deny your hair, we'll deny your skin, we'll deny your eyes. We deny you. We deny you when we accept you. We deny the ways in which you are not exactly us, by ignoring them."

Some of the blacks who "migrate" to the white side must prove their whiteness by violently disparaging of other Negroes.

Some blacks find that the experience of living as white is "a strain" that can prove too great.

Nella Larsen's novel *Passing* is about two women: Irene and Clare. Both women are light enough to pass for white, but only Clare has chosen to do so. When she meets Irene for the first time again in years on the roof of a fancy Chicago hotel, she tells her, "You can't know how in this pale life of mine I am all the time seeing the bright pictures of that other life of mine that I once thought I was glad to be free of . . . it's like an ache, a pain that never ceases."

XI. Consciousness

During my loneliest winter in Minnesota, I would wake up around four o'clock in the morning and go downstairs to a large auditorium that served as a student lounge. It was underused, though its massive windows opened out onto a quaint scene: a hill, a bridge, and a frozen lake. While the sun rose and the snow-covered world became white outside of this, the most stranded of all dorms, I watched films like *Last Tango in Paris*. The still, forbidding landscape outside amplified the fact that so many people around me were asleep.

Many of the people who moved to Minnesota from Somalia were refugees escaping brutal clan violence. In *Yesterday, Tomorrow,* one woman says: "We fled, locking up our family house as though we were going away for a weekend trip into the country."

According to the Minnesota Department of Natural Resources, "Minnesota, icebox of the nation, once sweltered in tropical heat. Minnesota, breadbox to the world, was once the barren scene of titanic mountain-building and volcanic activity. This same country has been covered by countless seas, slowly advancing, then ebbing. Later came the ice sheets. To read such a history stretches the human imagination and instills a new perspective on life."

When interviewed about the sudden surge in Nuer patients in her Minnesota hospital, one nurse proclaimed, "Who ARE these people and WHY are they here? If they can't speak English, WHY ARE they here?"

XII. Centripetal Force

The second set of exercises from the Ethiopian language book includes a set of requests that come across as frustrated and indecisive, as though spoken by a lover who knows they'll be left soon:

Hurry (pl.) 2. Listen. 3. Now go back. 4. Sit down (pl.) 5. Stop. 6. Buy some meat (for yourself). 7. Catch (pl.) the men. 8. Sleep (pl.) there. 9. Hit the door. 10. Go on. 11. This wall. 12. That (piece of) wood. 13. That river bed. 14. These fires. 15. Those keys. 16. These boys. 17. That tent over there. 18. Those huts in the distance. 19. Clean this spoon. 20. Cut this rope. 21. Take the other one (fem.) to Ahmed. 22. Give me those. 23. Look at those (masc.) over there. 24. Cook the food. 25. Straighten up the beds. 26. Put (pl.) the loads on the truck. 27. Whiten these shoes. 28. Bring a little oil and some sugar. 29. Call the other women and the girl.

When I was nine, I played the daughter, Tzeital, in a summer camp production of *Fiddler on the Roof.* The songs were imbued by a sorrow so deep that, at the time, it felt as mysterious and thrilling as the notion of sex or violence. I sang the lyrics over and over again to myself.

For example, in the song "Anatevka" the villagers lament each tiny facet of the life they are leaving: *a stick of wood, a piece of cloth.* That (piece of) wood. These fires. Those huts in the distance.

In Nuer culture, the name Choul is given to a child who has lost an older sibling to death. In the year 2000, at which point the book *Nuer Journeys, Nuer Lives* was published, Choul was the most common male name among the Nuer in Minnesota.

After finding a job in a slaughterhouse, a Nuer man explained, "I only know that in Africa I was always happy, and now I am always sad."

XIII. Genealogy

When spring came one year, I sat on the hill just underneath the red railings of the art building and read the poetry of Leopold Sedar Senghor. He said, "The African image is not an image by equation but an image by analogy, a surrealist image." For example, he writes, "The elephant is strength, the spider prudence; horns are the moon, and the moon is fecundity." One thing can be something else entirely without ceasing to be what it was in the first place.

As for the passing Negro, one expert, Mr. White, explains: "Most Negroes wish him well."

It was only 1946 when people were estimating that between 5 and 8 million persons in the United States who are "supposed to be white" have some amount of Negro blood. When forced to conjecture about the future, some experts, according to *Negro Digest*, predicted that eventually the Negro would "be absorbed."

In the novel *Passing*, one white-seeming woman notes of the other, "About the woman was some quality, an intangible something, too vague to define, too remote to seize, but which was, to Irene Redfield, very familiar."

Roccavivi, Italy

The Strongman and the Clown

offee spits at me from a small paper cup as I walk down the gangway in the airport. "Why does coffee spit?" I ask. My dad, who for as long as I can remember has been jotting down quotes in a thin beige notebook, says, "Coffee spitting, now that's a good opener." "Yeah, and I'm going to use it." My mom laughs. My father feigns disappointment. We are at the end of a layover in Ohio, on our seventh trip to Italy as a family.

During the layover my mom asks me to put some Icy Hot on her back, so we march to the nearest restroom. She waits for me to pee, standing near the sink where she has uncapped the Icy Hot. It looks like a stick of deodorant. A woman who has just washed her hands looks lost and my mom smiles sweetly, pointing to the paper towel dispenser with her trusty stick of Icy Hot. The woman makes it clear that she doesn't know what my mother is doing. My mom looks at me, puts the Icy Hot on the counter then says "I'm going to pee, watch this," and I entertain the thought that perhaps this woman thinks my mom is crazy, as I look unrelated to her—a black woman across the bathroom from a small white lady, who is constantly motioning to people with deodorant. When she gets back from using the bathroom, she bends her neck forward and I apply the salve.

"You know what I'm looking forward to?" She asks as we walk back to the gate. "Dinners. Are you writing down everything I'm saying?"

I know what she means because I too was there that night in Assisi when we ate pasta with truffles. I remember the way the food tasted, how we had a sense of discovery in our blood, as though we were scouting out new territory to settle for the strange nation we as a family composed. We visited a friend and I ran through her property, picking young, green apples from her trees. She was black, a dancer, and I want to say that house was full of hardwood floors, draping fabric, and mirrors. She was deeply artistic, living in what felt to be a forest. It was as though we'd made contact with a resident of a little known, distant moon.

Once we board the plane, it gets dark. We are surrounded, for a moment, by multiple screens of a glowing yellow topographical map of Ohio and Kentucky and Indiana. Light glances off my parents' held hands. The cartoon of a plane taking off into a blue and white sky plays as our own plane ascends into night.

One of the great tragedies of our early vacations to Italy was the loss of the Pinocchio dolls. My mother fell in love with the smooth red and green figures, and several were stolen from our suitcases. So for me, the Italian fairy tale is imbued into the memory of our vacations. As the story goes, a newly carved Pinocchio leaves home one day, waving sweetly to his father. Neither of them realize how far he must journey before he can come home again.

Pinocchio is the story of a puppet, yes. But it is also the story of a child who turned out differently from what his father had intended.

My mother was disowned by her father around the time she started dating my dad. As she tells it, he disowned her because she moved out of the family home to live with some friends at a time when Italian girls, even in Detroit, weren't allowed to leave the house without a husband. He died not long after this silence settled between them.

The greatest surge of Italians to move to the United States occurred during the period from 1870 until 1920. Four million Italians immigrated during this time. The poor economy after unification sent many young men away to forge out a new life for their families. My mother was not the only daughter of this migration who fell in love with a black man.

In *Jungle Fever*, Italian-American Angie Tucci gets punched and kicked by her father as punishment for her relationship with a black architect named Flipper Purify. He shouts after her not to come home with any "nigger babies." The verb *whale* means to "whip, flagellate, flog, hide, larrup, lash, scourge, stripe, thrash, wear out." My mother swears that her father didn't know she was dating a black man. "He would have been upset," she says. "But I think if he knew daddy he would have come around." He was not a bigot, from anyone's recollection. Any guest she brought into the house was to be treated with the utmost respect, and my mother's friends came from all kinds of backgrounds. If there wasn't enough food, it went to the guest first. She has little memory of him saying anything negative about other ethnic groups. But it was the sixties. In Detroit. There had been that riot.

This story wants to be one of redemption. Of a man who crawls onto a deserted beach, filled with anguish and regret. Some Anthony Quinn, breaking his fist in the sand with sadness over the loss of his daughter. But of course, it falls somewhere short of that. What we know for sure is that in 1922, a twenty-two-year-old with four-inch-tall hair as rugged as a rock cliff gazed out of a porthole in third class on a ship headed for Ellis Island. He wore the tattoo of a naked lady on his arm, which he'd gotten years before when the circus came to town. He may have known that once in America, he would become a boxer. He may have been planning to bury fruit trees in winter, and tie together cut branches coated in zinc in spring, to inspire the growth of hybrid fruit. He may have known that he would hunt for dandelions along the edges of his neighbor's property to use for salads and sautés. But surely he had no clue that the family he was about to start would move back across the Mediterranean with Africa in its blood.

It is 1985. This is my maternal grandmother's second trip to Italy with us. Her own parents emigrated from Calabria before she was born, but we are headed to central Italy, to the tiny house where her dead husband was raised. She is wearing her favorite color from head to toe, is reading a magazine, thick glasses propped onto the bridge of her nose. The color pink has a taste for me, the flavor of a lollypop I was eating before takeoff, but also a smell: my grandmother's body. Lubriderm lotion, natural odor, and perfume. Her right eye, stung by a bee when she was three years old, glances off to the side. I tear at a plastic bag with huge yellow earphones inside of it while eating unsalted potato chips from a health food store. The seat I am sitting in looks humongous as I punch at my pillow and lie down in my temporary fortress of comfort. My mother has the posture of a dancer as she offers me gum. Her face is all angles and shadow, huge eyes and high cheekbones. My father is busy recording all of this. I can see him only in the way that strangers respond to the camera, or in the way my mother smiles with her eyes.

The memory I have of this trip has more to do with a movement toward than it does with arrival. We sit together in pajamas in a small blue room in a hotel named Mozart. "What time is it?" My father asks. "It's four," my mother says, reading *It* by Stephen King. "That's how old I am," I announce. Suspended by jetlag, we skirt along the shore of morning. My grandmother sits upright, completely engaged with the task of tearing cardboard cutouts of Minnie Mouse from a dress-up book for a game I have abandoned. I crawl from one bed to another. My father's voice sounds exhausted. I may or may not have fallen asleep when my grandmother read to me from *Dr. De Soto* about a tiny mouse who worked as a dentist on all sorts of animals. There he'd stand, confidently working inside the jaws of a massive pig or donkey or fox, seemingly unafraid that he might be chomped or swallowed.

The plot of *Pinocchio* is familiar, in part, because it involves a man being swallowed by a whale. This brings us to think of the Book of Jonah. Jonah is trying to run away from a task that God has given him: to warn the wayward people of Ninevah that their town will be destroyed unless they ask for God's forgiveness. It is an action plot, in some ways, a divine car chase. Jonah runs from his duty, and God follows him with tempests and whales. It becomes harder to run when Jonah realizes that other lives are at stake.

When the boat he's boarded gets caught in a storm, Jonah tells a group of mariners, "Take me up, and cast me forth into the sea; so shall the sea be calm unto you: for I know that for my sake this great tempest is upon you." In an illustrated version of the King James Bible, there is a rendering of Jonah in the water. He is an old man, gazing to his right, and behind him like a shadow stands the great tail of a whale. It looks as though he is about to be swallowed. But he looks stubborn, willfully ignoring the presence lurking behind and beneath. This image in particular helps convey the moment I am so fascinated by: where my mother and her father seem to be suspended, chest deep in some story they've wandered into, not particularly innocent or guilty of much, but not prepared either to forget or forgive. In this snapshot of time, their relationship is forever about to be swallowed into a dream from which it might never wake.

A whale is a mammal. Synonyms for it include, giant, behemoth, leviathan, mammoth, monster. I was a child of the "save the whales" generation. To me, the term connotes a universe of gray, blue, and green. The kind of melancholy you'd find in a Miles Davis song or a museum. When I think of the sea creature who swallowed Jonah, or the whale from *Pinocchio* who swallowed a father and his long lost child, I don't see an angry monster like Maestro. I wonder about the whale's own longings and loneliness. Emotions for which his body becomes a metaphor.

In college, I took a course on Italian neorealism. Scenes from *L'Avventura, Roma Citta Aperta, La Terra Trema, Umberto D*, and *La Strada* mixed with sleepily muttered fairy tales and the particular pronunciation of an Italian man singing, "If you're going to San Francisco" as we sat in La Capriciosa's restaurant in Rome.

Of all the filmmakers, Michelangelo Antonioni and Federico Fellini captured my imagination the most. During one trip to Italy, I was reading a book of interviews with Fellini. I finished it one afternoon in the room of a pension, with the sound of Rome traffic floating through the red curtains along with pink light. That vacation was spent seeking Felliniesque visions in every alley, every fountain, every old man's iris.

Many of Fellini's films involve a circus — *The Clowns, La Strada, Juliet of the Spirits* — if not an outright production with clowns, at least some incarnation of touring eccentrics who visit small towns and, in passing, electrify the imagination. A tightrope walker or strongman.

When I think of those first trips to Central Italy where my grandfather grew up, I come up against the scene of us walking down a dirt road toward a fair or circus. Flickers of noise and the tungsten glow of an unseen tent strain at my memory, though this part is my invention. When I recently asked my mother about this memory, she told me that this wasn't a circus, it was a fair put on by the Communist Party. "It was funny," she said. "There was this horrible rock band."

We drove from Abruzzi to Il Castello de L'Aquila listening to *Phantom of the Opera* and picked blackberries along the edges of a castle. I spent hours with a frail woman named for a flower, who kidnapped me in order for us to have deep discussions while opening our way through a set of Russian dolls. My ninth birthday was ushered in by a chorus of Italian widows singing "Ave Maria," as they wove through the small, candlelit dining room carrying an ice cream cake from a nearby bar. My diabetic father ate a spoonful of cake, which at the time seemed to me a touching sacrifice to make in the name of celebration. Nobody was a contortionist or a clown, but the laws defining our reality had definitely shifted. The boundary we'd crossed, manned by security guards with machine guns and German shepherds at the Leonardo Da Vinci Airport, was also a spiritual threshold. An answer to our unasked questions: What would have happened if my grandfather hadn't died? What stories live on the other side of forgiveness?

My second favorite Fellini film, *La Strada*, was filmed, among other places, in L'Aquila and Abruzzi. I wonder how far he was from my grandfather's village when, in the early 1950s, Fellini had a chord strung up between two buildings to keep a tightrope walker suspended in the air. I imagine the sounds of laughter and awe hitting the valley walls, echoing like dancing light against the steep hills of Rocca Veccia.

A whale is like a mountain, that presence to which we have become accustomed. There it looms, quietly in the distance. But at any moment, the shape that was a landscape might start to move, water sluicing off the tail. In elementary school, we took a whale watching field trip. I vaguely recall the sound of people's voices as the enormous blue bodies slipped up and flipped over in the ocean. To be in the presence of such large bodies was exhilarating.

The first time I went to Italy by myself, it was by train. Every time I brought an old Pentax to my face to take a picture of the dark green valleys we twisted through in the ancient Alps, our train would enter a tunnel, and a woman across the aisle would begin to laugh with sympathy. I drank a coffee in Austria while waiting for the next train, and boarded again, a feeling of disbelief hastening my heartbeat. Sleek, white exteriors began to show more and more signs of dilapidation. Walls took in oranges and pinks, as though blushing. Filmic sweeps of Antonioni from my memory began to shuffle in with the real scene of a country shooting past the window. When the train began to move across the lagoon the colors of my memory started to whiten, as though what we were rocketing through was light or time.

I drank a half carafe of red wine that night, and ate a small pizza with soppresata. The feeling of being drunk and alone in Italy felt like a rite of passage, or at least I kept telling myself that as I walked tipsily along the thin, twisting streets. My pension was just around the corner from Piazza San Marco, and I wandered out in front of the Basilica. I stood facing the massive architectural wonder with my hands on my hips, as though if I stepped onto the right spot of pavement, I'd be properly transported back to the last time I'd been in this place.

When I was four years old, I ran around Piazza San Marco in pink Nikes, shrieking like a parrot. My grandmother instructed me on how to hold out the birdseed sold to tourists to attract the pigeons, but the onslaught of gray bodies never failed to send my fistful of seeds flying and me into a bullet of terrified motion. As an adult, I waded through the tourists' bodies, trying to imagine the square empty enough for my four-year-old self to make so many laps around it.

In Yin Yoga, there are poses that reach so deeply into joint and bone tissue that people begin to cry. Not just from pain. From a sensation that has been buried. Teachers say that this is due to the fact that the body holds anxiety and tension from years ago in its tissue, but we don't always stretch enough to release it. I have found myself, without expecting to, crying many a time on the yoga studio floor, without much understanding as to why, but feeling a deep well of emotion push through my blood and out of my body. Sometimes in these moments, I have the vague taste on my memory of a forgotten sadness, the gray day and sound of it flitting past my perception.

This is what it felt like when I walked to a certain place on the square, as though I'd moved into a hip opener and long lost pain had come gurgling out. A memory of my grandmother so pure, and so strong, rattled through me for the next few hours. I cried in front of the Basilica. I cried while looking at the gondolas on a tiny bridge. I cried up the stairs to my room. On the phone with my parents. And deep, deep into the night. The next morning I tried to shield my puffy eyes from the man who checked me out of my room, but it was futile. I spent the next few hours wandering around in the sun, almost anxious to leave, and boarded a train that afternoon before twenty-four hours had passed.

In *The Year of the Whale*, Victor B. Sheffer writes of the whale, "From the moment of its birth until its final hour, day and night, it hears the endless orchestra of life around its massive frame. Silence is an unknown thing." The whale hears with its body. "It feels the music, too, for water presses firmly on its frame — a smooth continuous sounding board."

In the Disney cartoon, Pinocchio's first adventure is to join Strombolli's circus. Something about the garish lights and clumsy, sexualized puppets turns the adventure surreal. He is a boy confronted for the first time with the hollow pleasures of adulthood, and this mounting shadow of evil becomes the driving tension in the story. As an audience, we are not waiting for him to fall in love or conquer a dragon, we are rooting for him to maintain his innocence. Our reprieve comes in the moments when his innocence is what connects him to other people. On stage, for example, he slips up, gets caught in a mess of string, and manages to make the audience laugh. This gives him honest joy.

In *La Strada*, Gelsomina is sold to a circus strongman by her extraordinarily poor family. She is an odd little person, with the temperament of a small child and the face, she is told, of an artichoke. During their act, Zampano and Gelsomina stand facing each other in black and white, a shirtless strongman and a painted clown. She surprises herself when she recites her lines and gets the audience to laugh. As it turns out, making people happy is right down her alley.

Zampano says that sensitive members of the audience might want to look away as he breaks the thick chain wrapped around his body with the muscles in his chest. Gelsomina is the only one in the crowd who seems even remotely ill at ease. When Zampano accidentally kills the circus Fool, she repeats the fact with astonishment, stuck in the moment when she rushed to the injured man's side. Her wide-eyed innocence in the face of true pain makes her a natural clown.

Once, while walking to a restaurant on my seventeenth birthday, my family saw an old man get hit by a younger man. When his head hit the cement with an audible clap, my mother wiggled forward in outrage. "No!" She called out. She went surprisingly close to the aggressor. "Don't do that to him," she said, as though she could make a case to have the moment removed from time. It seems sometimes that my mother reacts to violence and cruelty as though they are accidents. Aberrations in human nature, rather than the rule.

When she went to visit her father before he died, my grandmother told my mother not to go too close to his bed. "It's best not to upset him," she said. I can't conjure the expression my mother must have worn, hovering in the corner like a naughty child. Her father left the world that night, in the middle of their grudge.

They always had a stormy relationship. My aunt and uncles shout with laughter about the way my mother got along with their father when she was a teenager. They were like a Tom and Jerry act, Wile E. Coyote and the Roadrunner, a pair of stubborn creatures that were always engaged in some kind of face-off. When she was young, every night, she knocked over her water glass, and her father fumed with irritation. She refused to eat the roasted fowl for dinner on the day their pet ducks disappeared. When she was sixteen, her father got angry with her all the time for breaking curfew. "Kill me! Kill me! You're going to have to pay for the funeral!" She screamed once, tearing at her shirt. "Did I ever tell you about the time I hid in the shower?" She asks. If he ever did find out that she'd had a child with a black man, I imagine it would be further proof to him that his daughter was, by nature, an entity beyond his comprehension or control.

"What were you like as a little girl?" I ask my mother. "Skinny, curious, sensitive. I would get my feelings hurt easily. I always tried to please people. Shy. Talkative." "What did people say about you?" "I was a little actress. I was very dramatic."

I've noticed, of late, that a lot of comedic actors resemble the star of Fellini's *La Strada*, his beloved wife, Giulietta Masina. In *Happy Go Lucky*, for example, Sally Hawkins opens her eyes wide and purses her lips, working with religious zeal to get the people she loves to smile. As a child, I spooned out bowls full of tomato sauce that my mother and grandmother had set to simmering on the stove, then ran back to the television to watch the way Lucille Ball's eyes blazed, the way she opened her arms into a circle as a way of saying "pizza" in Italian, her vaudevillian tendency to march and masquerade. I only realize now that these expressions remind me of my mother. And while this penchant for drama and exaggeration may simply be a way of eliciting chuckles from the studio audience, in all of these women, there lives a quality of compassion. Theirs is an effort to shift the tone of a chaotic world. If only everyone could be happy, they seem to be saying. What if everything was going to be all right?

Walking down the street of her father's village one afternoon, my mother taps me on the shoulder with animation. "That's how my father would walk!" She says, pointing to her cousin, Duilio. She hurries forward to walk alongside the man, gathering her hands behind her back like Charlie Chaplain. She turns her head to wink at me before continuing along in what we know to be a charade. In her comedic disposition lives impossible hope; a mime's attempt at reckoning with the ghost.

"Where is my home?" Gelsomina asks Zampano. They are on the beach, miles off from her own seaside town. "Over there," he says, gesturing vaguely off into the distance. There is always, between them, a silent pressure, an invisible wrestling match between their different types of strength, between their quiet, carried burdens.

One year on Christmas, I received two novels by Thomas Wolfe, *Look Homeward, Angel* and *You Can't Go Home Again*. Knowing my parents, these books were chosen less for their content and more for their names. On the title page of the latter, my mother wrote, "You can always come home." This is not particularly surprising. My mother loves me with the blind loyalty of those Italian mothers you see in the movies. I don't think these characters are exaggerated. What I hear in this inscription about returning home is the converse truth she had to live with: at the mercy of all that silence, those pent up explanations, she could not go back.

At a certain point, the rest of the community began to know that my mom was dating my father. "How dare you shop so close to your mother's house," a family friend said when she saw my mother out for groceries one afternoon. Whether or not my grandfather knew about my father before he died still remains a question.

Not too long after my parents started dating, my father got a job in Los Angeles. My mother had no idea what to do with her future. She lost interest in becoming an occupational therapist because, the year she started, the program instituted a requirement that students dissect a cadaver. She had broken up with a sailor who went off to join the navy. A friend had invited her to live on the island of St. Thomas. "You could have been a redhead," she tells me. And I try to imagine feeling like myself as a white child, or whatever I would have been running along the beaches of the Caribbean.

Poised at the brink of decision, the twenty-two-year-old went with her mother to Quebec for the world's fair. This is the same fair where Africans were displayed in the late nineteenth century, and where the Eiffel Tower was first unveiled. The shifting blueprint for a great unknown stood before her as she traversed the streets of the foreign city in winter. Joining my father in Los Angeles would mean building a future for herself, inventing a life entirely from scratch. "Everything was underground," she says, still astonished at the thought of Montreal's winter architecture forty years later.

Of all her father's children, my mother's journey— this pose of contemplation before embarking upon an ocean of uncertainty— most resembled his own, despite the fact that they seemed completely incapable of understanding one another. She remembers of car rides with just the two of them, en route to the airport to visit her sister in Virginia or to a geology field trip, that they had nothing to say to one another. But they both ended up farther than any of their siblings from the house where they grew up.

Six months after I sat in a beat-up white Nissan in a Detroit U-Haul parking lot with my cousin Travis, looking at *Artforum* magazine and wondering with him, "How do people *go* to biennales?" I find myself in Venice, accidentally in time to see the 2011 biennale myself. The first artist I notice when I stroll in is a black American named Rashid Johnson, whose installation includes mirrored bookshelves and multiple copies of Bill Cosby's *Fatherhood*. The living room evoked here, in a Venetian arsenal, resembles my own: the Cosby books, the coffee table that is made of mirrors.

There is a video where girls drag their hands along the sand of the beach. There is a video where a blind Dominican man carries a legless Haitian woman around the city streets. There is a wax rendition of a famous sculpture melting. There is a simulacrum of a living room where a projected movie acts as a clock. There is a room full of giant, dreamlike stone figures that have been made by an artist for his dead

child. A video installation invokes an elevator and authentically pro-
vokes a sense of movement and vertigo.

At the elbow of one segment of the show, I walk out into a temporary
café. The sky is dark with inky clouds despite the fact that a white-hot
sun beats down from the other direction. It has just rained. Everyone
sits on chairs that remind me of white Play-Doh, amid bubble-stone
lamps, under a giant iron pulley. We are at the water, there is a gon-
dola bobbing idly in the Pirates of the Caribbean–colored lagoon.
People are drinking wine in plastic cups, espresso in Illy paper cups,
and there is a woman with white hair eating ice cream. We are starting
to look at each other like art. The sculpture of a giant whale lies in the
sand off to the side. It is as if we have, by the end, all entered into the
same dream. I can hear the strands of Nino Rota, the delighted chords
of whimsy as a woman dreams up some scene while dozing on the
beach in a Fellini film: a cluster of children rolling giant wheels, men
in white, fragments from the subconscious parading onto the shore,
arriving from or embarking upon the body of the ocean together.

In Fellini's *Juliet of the Spirits*, Giuletta Masina's character dreams
that a man in a red robe is whispering to her. He asks her to help him
drag a rope from the ocean. She looks up to see a boat full of people
with strange markings. A black man with a beard is standing in profile, holding a sword, and he looks back at the beach toward her. In
another dream, a door opens to a room full of people frozen in time.
There is a black man with sticks holding his dreadlocked hair in what
looks to be a Japanese bun, a white woman with white face paint, a
short white man in his underwear with his mouth open, women in
veils. I wonder how blackness lived inside my grandfather's subconscious. If one kind of blackness ever held the place of another.

It occurs to me that the world's fair and to an extent, the Venice
Biennale are visions of the future, attempts to explain the journey out
of our current set of troubles and conflicts. There is an enormous
amount of reference to war and violence. Each piece is its own version of a map that could guide us from the country of one mind to
the country of another.

In order to get to the bus for the airport, I ride a vaporetto in Venice
from Palanka to Tronchetto just before four o'clock in the morning. I
almost miss the 3:48 departure time, and sit breathing heavily with my
backpack taking up most of the seat behind me while its straps brace

my shoulders like two strong hands. Listening to "Sketches of Spain" for the duration of the ride through the dark makes me feel sure that Miles Davis composed the album in the middle of the night. As we swing around the curves of the lagoon, I feel as though I am hearing the music for the first time. The confluence of his music with the way the boat moves slowly in that silence gives me a new sense of rootedness in Italy. Jazz seems at times like a form of citizenship: the black man's passport to Europe. As we ebb up against the adagio, moving exactly along the logic of its liquid phrasing, I stake new claim to the country of my grandfather's birth.

In Hal Whitehead's *Voyage to the Whales*, he writes: "Many have tried to describe the song of the humpback, but it is more than 'sonorous groans' or 'unearthly wails.' They use the highest notes we can hear, the lowest, and all in between, to construct an elegant adagio."

As I watch *Pinocchio* again, I am struck by how old Giapetto is. He is a white-haired man in a house full of clocks, surrounded by the sound of ticking. When he carves from wood the son he never had, his loneliness is transformed from a vacancy to a solid form. Later on, trapped inside the belly of the whale, he floats inside a universe as expansive as the sky: a place where time expands and contracts, where light is not always a reflection of the sun. Here we can see the way his life must have felt on land as his solitude is magnified. This story might not be about the boy at all but rather about the sad fantasies of a man who, toward the end of his life, has come to question the notion of home if the house is empty.

On our seventh trip to Italy as a family, we traveled by ship. When we boarded, we came to find that the ship was named *Freedom*, so my mother sang protest songs and clapped. Some days I would go to the ship's gym and lie in the sauna to warm up, as I was constantly cold. I had a porthole all to myself, where I could confront the enormity of the ocean alone. This was a preoccupation of mine. It would be a shame, after all, to go to sea without admitting to the scope of it. It was hard to find these moments, where I could let the illusion of comfort offered by all-day buffets and talk of postcards dissolve like a haze and stare at the horizon, sensitive to the fathoms below.

My appreciation for the ocean comes mostly from elementary

school. We spent quite a bit of time studying whales. For weeks we listened to recordings of them calling after each other, watched the fictional characters on *Voyage of the Mimi* desalinate sea water while stranded on an island, where they studied the ways whales migrated and fed. More than species names or behavioral patterns, a more subtle lesson stays with me from that curriculum: the ocean is a lonely drift. But it is a place where sound travels faster than in air. The voice of a whale takes less time to reach his calf. Beneath our ship, I imagined that the vibration of whale song spread out like sleep between bodies, a moaned note with the same texture as love or heat. One night our ship shook as violently as an airplane flying through a storm.

There is footage of my father driving through Paris. To the unseen cameraman, he admits: "I know it's *touristy*. But I'd like to see the Eiffel Tower. I've never seen it." There is something so young in this confession, a kind of wonder. I feel heartened by it, and too, it makes me think of the father-in-law he never had. When my mother's father was alive, he traveled around the country to do construction projects. He worked on the Empire State Building and the Golden Gate Bridge. A mutual appreciation for architecture flashes through my mind as one of the things they never got to share together. My father swears he saw his wife's mother walk down the hall in our apartment in Los Angeles on the night she died in a hospital in Detroit. What, then, might he and his father-in-law have looked like and spoken of, tucked together in private conversation?

Sheffer describes what it is of whale watching that makes the concept so calming to me. "In the still air of the afternoon the little sounds are few and far between, like the whisperings of a desert land, though the sea below is all aquiver with subdued noise—the ultrasounds of a thousand whales communicating with one another and holding their group together by invisible chords." I've wondered, these days, if we can let go better our own thought patterns or grievances when we imagine them as though from a distance. Not unlike the angels perched on top of skyscrapers in Wim Wenders's film *Wings of Desire*, for whom the most troubling thoughts of human beings can be heard as a cacophony of murmur, the sweet, soft symphony of our anguish and regret. Emulating angels, we might be able to allow memories and relationships to become languid, like a song that starts out so sad but rattles as it rises.

In 2002, Roberto Benigni made a live-action version of *Pinocchio*. Long before this, Fellini described Benigni as "light, very funny, moonstruck, mysterious; a good dancer, a mime artist, who made people laugh and cry. He has the fascination of characters in fairy tales or the great literary works. He makes any landscape believable; he is a friend of ogres and princesses and talking frogs. He's like Pinocchio."

In Benigni's version of the film, it's clear that the puppet's journey to become a real boy is an accelerated experience of growth. As proof of his new maturity, he develops a sweet composure. He is dedicated to his father, works long hours at a farm to earn a single glass of milk to feed him. Through redemption, the scene of what could be a deathbed is transformed into the location of physical and emotional renewal.

One of the excursions for the cruise was to Pompeii. Our tour guide, with an uncanny resemblance to Roberto Benigni, had a kind of fantastic boredom about him. This was evident in his rumpled attire, and in the tired recitation of facts that came streaming out of his mouth. But he also wore pink, and had a wry smile, which insinuated perhaps that it was not the world that bored him, but the way in which he had to present it to a bus full of tourists who take in entire cities — the city of his birth — in a few hours, from behind panels of glass. He amused me, and also, he kept looking at me. Not with a leer, but with the kind of recognition you might not know the foundations of, but you'd just as soon accept. If you feel kindred, then, hey, so do I.

My father and I asked the tour guide to hold the bus for a moment while my mother used the bathroom, and we stood chatting with him in the sun as the bus full of tourists idled. "What did you do before this?" my father asked. "I a-was a teacher." "What age?" "Teenagers." The cell phones and the flirting and the ignoring just about ruined his soul. But he had to make a living, so he got involved with the tourist trade. "What'd you do before that?" my father asked. "I went-a to school." "What did you study?" I chimed in. "Jean Cocteau. A French writer." This was perhaps the most interesting fact I'd heard all day. "I just saw one of his films back at home," I said. "Yes," our guide smiled. "He made films as well."

Back on the bus I realize what it is that makes this man so much more than his bored facade. I replay scenes from *The Testament of Orpheus* in my head as we mount a hill, verging closer to Pompeii. Cocteau's black-and-white reel of images plays against the color of the world outside: backward-flowing water and disappearing angels superimposed against the blue ocean, small cars, and tall buildings. The magic of Cocteau hums for him, perhaps, beneath the humdrum of this silly institution, this cheap but lucrative stand-in for true curiosity.

After wandering through the ruins, staring into the empty baths, trying to put life back into the petrified bodies dually killed by Mount Vesuvius and preserved by her cooled lava, after studying the walls of the ancient brothel with its "instructive" tableaux, we prepare to reboard the bus. We are early this time, and chat again with our driver. "You are a-lucky to have two women," he tells my father. "And you? Do you have two women in your life?" my mom asks. "Since one month. My daughter is just born." He turns to me, without wryness or mystery, and gazes straight into my eyes. "She looks a-like you. This is why I am so often looking at you. My wife, she is from Colombia. She has a-skin like yours." He points, this time, to my father. "We name her Naima, after a John Coltrane song."

Cocteau says that beauty is always the result of an accident. Somewhere inside me, the fist of fear that I've always held, clasped in the notion that my grandfather wouldn't have wanted to know me, begins to loosen. Our family's strange little unit has been tucked and rooted more firmly in the soil of something irrefutably Italian — amid bodies more ancient, even, than the one in my grandfather's grave.

A homeless Senegalese painter named Joseph once told me something odd. We were standing in Paris, in the cave of his temporary studio — a nook between buildings tucked away from the traffic where his paintings were leaned and stacked. I wanted to buy something from him, but he refused to speak to me straight. He was drunk, and spoke in mystic fragments. He said, "Before he died, your grandfather cried my name."

Both my grandfathers had reason enough to do this. My paternal grandfather was named Joseph, and my mother's father had a Joseph for his eldest son. This moment gave me reason to consider the scene of both grandfathers on their deathbeds. What could have been said in the absence of a listener? On his deathbed, Fellini cried for Giuletta.

A whale, though not an elephant, is a lurking presence. An indication of the depth that the surface of a story cannot afford to utter. And yet there is the notion of these underwater moans. The way the truth blooms somewhere, in a last breath or underwater. Victor B. Sheffer imagines the sonic history of a whale: "Today he hears another sound like an interstellar cry. It starts as an eerie moan without dimension, formless. It rises to a scream and then fades away, trembling, descending, echoing faintly, leaving the little calf frozen. From whence the cry? It never comes again. Perhaps a creature from the deeps as yet unknown to man? Perhaps an ordinary animal, far beyond its normal haunts? Perhaps a silent creature forced to break its silence by some agonizing pain?" I've had occasion to wonder whether emotions, the ones that come on strong and strange with little provocation, are rippling out from the past or latitudinally, the fog of shame or longing or laughter floating around the atmosphere, catching in us briefly like ancestral whispering.

Once upon a time, my grandmother, father, mother, and I got off a train in a small Italian town. We visited the small room, a cellar really, where my grandfather lived with all his siblings. Our cousins fed us strawberry wine. Olive trees waved in the wind like green ash. "My father had hands as hard as rocks," my mother remembers, "from all that work." So did Micucci, his best friend from childhood, whom we went to see during the course of our visit. Scientists cannot calculate how long it takes for a father's wish for redemption to travel across the threshold of death to reach the waiting heart of his child. But when the rock-hard hands of a short, surrogate Italian slammed up against my father's head, it was for the purpose of drawing him closer. He gave my father a kiss on each cheek and welcomed him inside.

London, England

Silencing Cassandra

ement throws heat back after a ferocious summer afternoon. It's after six in the evening, and as I walk alongside my dog, thin wisps of vertical, gray rain and curly beards of darkening clouds miles away in the mountains begin to glow, cayenne stained by sunset. A song by the British singer P. J. Harvey plays in my head, and England comes to life like a carousel between me and the scene that surrounds.

I don't realize until watching the news later that London is in flames. Neighborhoods I remember strolling through to take pictures and buy reggae are being patrolled by angry teenagers and armed policemen.

A friend tells me to watch the newscast of a BBC interview. In it, a West Indian man who is identified as a writer and broadcaster is being asked to explain why the riots are happening. He is bald, standing in front of a charred corner building that is being hosed down by an invisible firefighter. The man being interviewed looks down as he listens to the blonde woman who sits in a studio on the other half of the split screen. "Are you shocked by what you've seen?" she asks.

He reminds me of my grandmother as he spits out responses that, to the impatient ear, might sound pause filled and garbled. He is not shocked. He has been living in London for fifty years. "What I was certain about, listening to my grandson and my son was that something very serious was going to take place in this country. Our political leaders have no idea. The police have no idea. But if you looked at young blacks and young whites with a discerning eye and careful hearing, they have been telling us. And we would not listen." These words call to mind an essay that Henry Louis Gates Jr. wrote in 1976 about the dance halls or "blues parties" in black London, where "the prevailing emotion is 'the cool,' an ice blue cool. No one speaks, there is no laughter." He goes on, "These blues are not happy or sad, but limbo — limbo plus despair. And the sounds, the sounds blare at an almost unimaginable level, deadening the nerves, killing response. Anesthetization of the soul."

"Excuse me, Mr. Howe, Mr. Howe, if I could just interrupt you for a moment." The reporter does not want to listen to whatever it is that she and everyone else has not been listening to in the first place. She asks if he condones the riots. There is a delay in their connection, which enhances the tension between them. ". . . I condone? If I, of course I do not." He tries, again, to bring up the reason that the riots have occurred. "There is a man called Mark Duggan." Howe's voice becomes shrill. "He has parents, he has brothers, he has sisters, and few yards away from where he lives a police officer blew his head off, blew his head off, blew his face off with a . . ." The reporter stops him.

"Now Mr. Howe." Her timing is not clumsy, it is strategic, launched at the exact moment when it will inspire the most acute sense of futility and irritation. He asks her to let him finish, but she interrupts. In my head, P. J. Harvey sings, "These, these, these are the words, the words that maketh murder."

Harvey's album *Let England Shake* was released earlier in the year. In a song entitled simply, "England," she sings of the social or spiritual stagnation of the British people. It is not the words but the sound that makes this slow, slurred song so emotional. The sound of a female voice in the background sings the lament of a person in mourning, half hysterical alongside Harvey's exhausted yowl. In order to prepare for the album, Harvey researched the experience of war, intrigued especially by the firsthand accounts of soldiers and civilians. In an interview, she says, "I think as a creative artist it's crucial to be open — to feel. You can't do it with a closed heart. You almost have to hand over your soul to that action." Each track lets, like a needle in a vein, the blood out of a sick body, extracting a kind of poison. After weeks of listening, I still feel unemptied by it.

The grating, naked vulnerability expressed in this music is not unlike a ritual Anne Carson describes in her essay "The Gender of Sound." Choes was practiced in ancient Greece during the festival of Dionysus. In it, a woman is chosen to perform an act of verbal expression. "She is the woman," Carson writes, "who discharges the unspeakable things on behalf of the city."

When I first started teaching at a university, I was twenty-six years old. On the morning that I arrived for my first class, the students were standing in the hall. They explained that we could not get into the room until the teacher arrived. I pushed through the crowd and opened the door, and they stared at me as though I hadn't heard them.

A week earlier, during our orientation training, we had been told to adopt a teaching "persona," and we were given ideas of how to flesh out this role for ourselves. My persona involved little other than wearing a necklace of inch-thick pink beads that I had bought at a cheap chain store in Munich while visiting my friend that summer. Dressing up felt foreign to me, and this concession toward formality was about all I could muster at that time to pronounce my authority to the rest of the room. I spent almost the entire time behind the chemistry station that stood close to the front of the room.

By the end of the semester, I felt a great sense of connection to the class. One girl made me a mix CD of bands that I loved, and I listened to it every night. A football player had established himself, with full acceptance from the rest of the class, as the most promising poet among us, and we applauded his freewrites daily. I felt so enamored of them that I was baffled. How could you feel this much love toward an entity that is not your family? I was grateful and scared and exhausted.

At the same time, I felt nervous navigating the line between my true self and my teacher self. Toward the end of our time together, upon the recommendation of a colleague, I shared part of an essay that I was working on. It was an emotional scene about how distant I felt from my nephew's experience in prison. As eighteen-year-olds (mostly) in a university class, they were warned from the start that the material they were presented with may be "adult," so I had no qualms, at first, about quoting the documentary *Scared Straight*. After all, the 1970s footage seemed so archaic, I couldn't imagine that it would be shocking to them. But they weren't looking at the feathered hair and afros on the pompous teenagers, they were looking at me. The scene in particular that I quoted included words like "fucked up the ass." More than a cussing teacher, though, I was an estranged aunt, forcing herself to imagine what kind of violence might be inflicted on her nephew. When they were silent at the end of the reading, I began to cry.

When I was in second grade, my teacher broke into tears. A classmate and I had been relentlessly making fun of the way she blinked one day when she had something in her eye. I loved her dearly, and was shocked that I had the ability to hurt her. "You should be careful not to hurt a person's feelings," she had told us then. Years later, I told my class, "You should say something when someone shares something with you." Both moments stand out as accidents, unintentional expressions of vulnerability in an environment that relies on the maintenance of total composure. The activity that I had chosen to do immediately following my reading was, appropriately enough, filling out course evaluations. I handed the packet to the girl with the Alaska sweatshirt and left the room.

Later that day, I got e-mails from a few students apologizing, saying that they felt bad for making me upset. They just hadn't known how to react. Stripped down, without a necklace of persona, we all found ourselves stuttering without a script.

After Darcus Howe begins to describe the death of Mark Duggan, the BBC reporter cuts him off. "We don't know what happened to Mr. Duggan," she says. This is how history gets warped and erased, I realize, as I feel a flash of white hot anger wash through my body. "We are going to wait for the police report on it." My heart is beating fast.

The volume on his microphone is lowered, but an angry Mr. Howe is speaking with animation. All I can hear of this muted rant is: "Mr. Duggan is dead." The reporter doesn't find this useful, and pushes on with a new point. Suddenly, she wants to know again about the young black men. What is wrong with them again? Once he realizes that she's asked a new question, Howe pauses and begins to respond.

He speaks of his grandson, whom he describes as an angel. As soon as the boy started to mature, the police started to harass him. "I asked him the other day, apropos of the sense that something was going seriously wrong in this country. I said, 'How many times have the police touched you?' He said 'Papa, I can't count, there have been so many times.'" Inaudible remarks continue. The tenderness he feels for his grandson is apparent in the way his voice is cracking.

It is at this point that the conversation turns into a fight. "Mr. Howe, that may well have happened, and if you say it did then I am not to gainsay you, but that is no . . . that is not an excuse to go out and riot and cause all sorts of damage as we have been seeing over the course of the last few days."

He asks her where she was in 1981. She avoids the question. He tries to speak again. "I don't call it rioting, I call it an insurrection of the masses of the people. It is happening in Syria, it is happening in Clapham, it is happening in Liverpool, it is happening in Port of Spain, Trinidad, that is the nature of an historical moment."

"Mr. Howe."

"That is the . . . I'm listening."

"Mr. Howe if I could just ask you, you are not a stranger to riots, are you? You have taken part in them yourself."

As he repeats her words, it takes him a moment to absorb what she has just said. He slows. "I have never taken part in a single riot. I have been on demonstrations that ended up in a conflict. And have some respect for an old West Indian Negro and stop accusing me of being a rioter. Because I don't want to communicate abusively. You just sound idiotic. Have some respect."

"Mr. Howe."

"I have grandchildren —"

"Thank you very much for joining us. Darcus Howe."

The reason that the riots in London in August of 2011 started was because the man who Howe referenced, Mark Duggan, was shot by the police. He ran from them after they followed him under suspicion that he was a drug dealer and gang member. Reports now say that it was in the chest, not the face, but he was indeed shot and killed instantly.

"Why are all the bodies black?" the man asked, shaking his knee. He had started out the semester in the front row, and had made his way slowly to the very back. It was my third semester of teaching at a community college. The campus was in a part of Tucson that I'd been warned not to enter by a wealthy psychologist living in the foothills because she'd read somewhere that blacks and Latinos don't get along.

My experience was, on the contrary, quite positive. I enjoyed working with older students, and this semester most of the people who made it to the evening course were at least thirty, in the middle of one life path, hoping to start or shift to another. The first unit had gone well, and I thought I'd bring in the photography of Lorna Simpson for some visual analysis. Simpson's early work focuses quite a lot on the black, female form: an anonymous female's back facing the camera above captions that create a narrative or conceptual framework for the figure above. The piece we were looking at involved a woman who held in one hand a plastic gallon jug, and in another, a silver one, which had inspired a conversation about memory, history, slavery.

The student who spoke was Native American. He was the product of two tribes. Though we had gone through many gay, Latino, black, and white authors and artists, not once had we read the work of a Native American author. "I just don't understand why it's only black people," he said.

I had made friends with this class. Of the five rows, two were full of allies looking at me with sympathy, looking at him with concern, which bolstered my sense that I was not necessarily doing anything wrong. I asked him to expand on his thoughts, but he refused. It seemed obvious to me at that moment that my identity as a young black female teacher might have something to do with his irritation. It seemed obvious to me that our social roles made the moment go one way instead of another.

In the book *The Presence of the Actor*, playwright Joseph Chaikin writes, "We compose ourselves from the cultural models around us. We are programmed into a status hunger. Once we have masked ourselves with the social image suitable to a type, we enter the masquerade of the setup. Even the masquerade of our ethnic and sex roles permeates our life so thoroughly that many of us are afraid to give them up. In giving them up we fear we would be giving up our identity, and even life itself."

"Bow your head," someone suggests. This is the first step to dancing ska. "Swing your arms, shake your hips. Now do a-this!"

Another YouTube video shows an old program with instructions for the dance. "This is ska. Original and indigenous. The music of guitar, saxophone, trumpet, bass, and drums. These instruments are playing a monotonic, grassroots rhythm. This beat has taken Jamaica by storm. And it's quickly spreading to the rest of the world. Now, what is the authentic style of this new dance craze? Let's take a look shall we?"

Throughout the four basic steps described in the video, the camera features four different pairs of dancers performing the isolated gesture being described at the time. The instructions certainly do give a sense of what it is that these bodies are doing: "Keep the beat with the upper half of the body, bowing forward with a straight back, and a slight bend in both knees. At the first bow, the arms extend to the sides. At the second bow, the arms cross in front. The body straightens up at the change of arms from one position to the other."

But knowing how to do these movements seems like a fraction of the reason that the music and the dance have such a hypnotic appeal.

"People who don't suffer like us can't perform that sound — it's a sufferer's sound. No middle-class Jamaicans can play the music we play; it's a ghetto sound that we play out of instruments, real suffering ghetto sound. It sound happy, yes, for it's relief!" one musician explains in *Solid Foundations*, by David Katz. Don Drummond of the Skatalites was said to blow "an iron that was black and blue, Peter Pan for lost Black man."

A hurricane sent Jamaicans to look for work in London after World War II. Apartments for rent wore signs that said "No Blacks. No Dogs. No Irish," which kept the possibilities for housing slim. The bombed-out wreckage of a neighborhood like Notting Hill would have to do. Living conditions never promised to be plush. The Jamaican photographer Charlie Philips shot a picture of a crumbling building with white words painted across the brick: "Princess Patience Blues." Another photographer, Armet Francis, explains of the first wave of immigrants to London that Jamaica "is not just a warm feeling as it is for those of us who grew up here. Jamaica, for them, is an alive thing, but in the form of a memory they nurture through dances and through the market place and especially through the church. They can smell nyah-nyah or oily oily, or shop for cassava and plantains, then close their eyes and see Jamaica. What else can they do, mahn — be British?"

When I was in high school, the coolest girl in my class played a bit role in *Revenge of the Nerds II*. Many of my classmates' parents worked in the arts or in Hollywood, so the social hierarchy was a little screwy compared with what I knew of the "real" America—full of artsy photography buffs, brilliant improvisational actors, and aspiring poets. My high school was not even particularly liberal, but it was all-girls, and I didn't meet a cheerleader until I was well into my twenties. After deciding against the college where, my guidance counselor warned me, "everyone wears black and smokes a pack a day," I went to a small liberal arts college with no Greek system. Students spoke of our football team as though it were a ghost that, sure, years ago people may have encountered but no one alive today had ever seen. Frisbee and its winter complement, "broom-ball," got much more play; bulky wool socks were worn under sandals once the temperature dropped below freezing; and the library at eleven at night was as bustling as any off-campus house party.

When I first came to graduate school at a big university, I got a sudden crash course in big university living. I lived across the street from Fraternity Row. On one of the first weekends spent in my new apartment, I peeked out the blinds to see members from the SWAT team running through my driveway, in the direction of the gunshots I thought I'd heard a bit earlier. I found out later that some frat boys had exchanged words with "two young Latino boys" in a Del Taco before the guns were drawn. The story was strangely absent from the news, but one of my students had almost gotten shot in the encounter and filled me in.

Every week or so, my neighbor would rent out our driveway for football parking. People in red shirts would start walking through my neighborhood, carrying coolers and lawn chairs, and I would lock myself inside and draw the blinds as if the glare from all that red hurt my eyes. At all hours of the day, expensive cars full of young Caucasian boys cruised down the main drag with rap blasting out the windows. There were those infamous themed parties I'd heard about in conversations about reality TV, like "Thugs and Hos," but one of the fraternities took things a bit further with the "Come as Your Favorite Black Person" party. Growing up, I had thought of campuses like this as twisted, fantasy kingdoms, and it was jarring to realize that this was not a place where the social outcasts ultimately prevailed to the tune of a Queen power ballad. Living near the campus of a true party school was like a lucid dream. I had wandered onto the set of a mockumentary only to find that it was real.

So it was not terribly surprising when, a few years into teaching there, I was confronted by a student who was starting to have trouble with all "the lies." I started nodding my head so ferociously that the student started to look at me with narrowed eyes, as though I were exaggerating for his benefit. "Nobody talks about anything real," he complained, pacing around the room after class with noticeable anxiety. I'd noted, early on in the semester, that this student had a lot of promise. His comments and writing had a kind of raw clarity about them. But over the course of the semester, his contributions to class discussion became more and more awkward and disjointed. Students who used to laugh along with his witty remarks weren't sure what to do anymore when he spoke out of turn.

I did what I could to distract the class when my student said things they did not understand. They began to look to me for guidance instead of laughing when he made a joke that fell flat. The fact that his skin was brown only seemed to intensify the room's uncertainty about him. Everyone started to seem much younger, including myself. I felt the urge to look behind my shoulder for the real adult in the room, and I was shaken to realize it had to be me. For a time, I entered into a repartee with him so that the rest of the class might be tricked into thinking his jokes were just as funny as they'd always been. Couldn't they see? But when he slammed his books down onto the table after arriving late one afternoon, it was impossible to pretend that everything was OK. The glare of normalcy was starting to weigh down on him, and every word out of his mouth was an expression of his exhaustion. Eventually, he stopped coming to class at all. As happens often when a young man of color eventually stops coming to class, I felt as though I had failed him as a teacher, let him slip through the fingers of a system built to see boys like him fall. I still wonder what I could have done differently.

Recently, someone told a story about a Zen Buddhist who was invited to visit a man in a mental institution. The man was feared to be schizophrenic, and everyone had to keep convincing him that he was not Jesus Christ, as he claimed to be. The Buddhist took a different approach. "I hear that you're a carpenter," he said to the man. While they spoke, the man built the Buddhist a bookshelf. Soon afterward, he was released. According to Buddhism, all perception is an illusion anyway, so what was the harm?

In the 1967 text *The Politics of Experience*, the renowned but controversial psychotherapist R. D. Laing includes a narrative about a sculptor named Jesse Watkins who had a "psychotic episode." It was an exquisite experience, providing a kind of clarity the likes of which the man had never seen. But it was, too, terrifying, and a part of him felt anxious to return to the state of normalcy that he'd been living in before, even if the scope of that state felt somewhat limited. Luckily, he was treated with kindness by his loved ones. And he was sure of one thing. If someone had locked him up, closed the door to his padded cell, he may never have been released from his break with reality. He would have been in a state of total withdrawal from the world. Laing concludes, *"Can we not see that this voyage is not what we need to be cured of, but that it is itself a natural way of healing our own appalling state of alienation called normality?"* (emphasis original).

When I was sixteen, I looked at the white sphere of sun through the Santa Monica smog and experienced a jolt of insight. It began with logic: if the sun looked small, and it was so much larger than the earth, then I was smaller than an ant. I was as insignificant as dust. This simple shift in self-perception drove me into a state of absolute euphoria. I stood in the kitchen, explaining a new religion to my mother. "Something about the sun. How the sun is the center of . . . I mean how we are all . . ." She nodded patiently, and could perhaps have been wondering if I was on drugs, which I was not. "I think there are religions like that already, sweetheart," she said, undeterred from her chopping. I went to my room and wrote down every thought that came to my head in a red Pentel marker, while listening to Paul Simon's 1986 album *Graceland*. It took me days to come off of this high. When a friend complained, the next afternoon, about a disagreement with a teacher, I did a series of back walkovers, as though I had suddenly turned into Leslie Caron. I felt a sense of great dread that I was sliding away from this feeling. Flickers of it have returned, on pot highs and while encountering certain films or pieces of art, but nothing compares to the way I was able to see my role in the universe explode that hazy afternoon.

Joseph Chaikin writes, "'Reality' is not a fixed state. The word 'reality' comes from the Latin word *res*, which means 'that which we can fathom.'"

What haunts me is that I could see that my student was right, that we were living in a massive delusion, where people seemed literally to be wearing costumes and stage makeup. But I couldn't do anything to comfort him about it. I didn't know how to tell him that it was possible to see the illusion without feeling warped by it. To play your role in the game while fully accepting that it was fake, without feeling like you were going to lose your mind.

I went to London not long after the attacks on the Pentagon and Twin Towers. The news was still playing footage of falling bodies and of the still columns that erupted, one at a time, into an orange cloud, outrageously beautiful against the perfect blue sky. I didn't exactly intend to be in England. The program I'd applied to in Cuba had fallen through. I was running out of time, and if I was going to go anywhere it pretty much had to be on the English department's drama-themed trip to London. I had hoped for my study abroad experience to be slightly more far flung but soon took to London with a voracious appetite. Walking around filled some part of me that turned out to be insatiable. Buskers. Reading on the Tube. Movies at the Barbican. People watching at the National Film Theatre. The time was not wasted on me. The two plays we attended each week were an obligation. I had no real interest in theater. But the pomp and circumstance of going out to such cultural events felt luxurious. Every now and then, I stayed awake through the entirety of a show.

I didn't think I was interested in British culture, but I was interested in the way that the British experienced race. One of my favorite films was Mike Leigh's 1996 film *Secrets and Lies*. In it, Marianne Jean-Baptiste plays a successful black Brit who seeks out her birth mother after the death of the woman who adopted and raised her. She finds, to her surprise, the struggling, white Brenda Blethyn, whose bottom lip seems to be in a constant quiver. During one scene at a café, Blethyn lets out a convulsive cry, gasping and snorting out the word *Sweetheart* over and over again. The explosion of her voice, more and more amorphous as her sobs begin to rack her, still repeats in my memory the way a song would.

In "The Gender of Sound," Anne Carson writes, "Ololyga, eleleu, alalazo. These words do not signify anything except their own sound. The sound represents a cry of either intense pleasure or intense pain."

I arrived late when my class went to see the Wooster Group's version of Phaedra: *To You, the Birdie!* The docent who stood by the door of the theater while I waited for intermission tried to explain the plot to me, pointing out the characters on a small monitor. But when I entered the theater for the second act, these directives felt irrelevant. The set was a collage of technological equipment: large screens, small screens, projected images, a badminton court, a DJ-like soundstage where the garbles of the woman playing the protagonist, Phaedra, were translated by a male narrator. What I remember most is the sound of breaking glass, which coincided with the sound of Phaedra's hysterical screams.

Chaikin writes, "Because we live on a level drastically reduced from what we can imagine, acting promises to represent a dynamic expression of the intense life. It is a way of making testimony to what we have witnessed—a declaration of what we know and what we can imagine."

One day when I was in elementary school, the air must have started to darken prematurely. A strange smell of smoke that wasn't barbecue started to waft through Culver City to our street of weeping trees. My father was probably already in South Central, taking a photograph of a blurred man on a motorcycle who was looking behind him toward a building that had caught fire. I don't know if we were sent home early from school that day. All I remember is the empty classroom, and the sense that something was happening somewhere. That the line between here and there was fragile.

In *City of Quartz*, Mike Davis writes that before the Los Angeles riot of 1992, policemen who believed that they were doing their jobs began accidentally killing black men with chokeholds, and blaming these deaths on the victims' anatomy. Black and Latino teenagers who went to a wealthy neighborhood park to play basketball were thrown onto the pavement and taunted. An apartment building under suspicion of drug and gang activity was ransacked, plastered with graffiti stating, among other things, "LAPD Rules!" And residents were handcuffed. They were told to whistle the theme song to *The Andy Griffith Show* while being beaten with flashlights. It was not until Rodney King's beating by police was caught on tape that people began to throw stones.

After the Watts Riots of 1965, Martin Luther King Jr., Bayard Rustin, and Andrew Young went on a tour of the areas affected. They were approached by victorious young people, shouting, "We won! We won!" When the civil rights leaders asked them why, they said, "We won because we made them pay attention to us!"

In high school, two of my closest friends told me that they had "driven through" South Central, because they felt curious and obligated to know this part of the city. I myself visited, to my memory, only once as a child. We went to the home of my father's friend Bobby, and it was physically very difficult for me to remain upright. I felt the constant pull to crouch onto the floor rather than standing in full view in front of the living room windows, in case there was a drive-by. It was not until I was an adult, visiting home well after college, that I walked down Central Avenue. By then, most blacks had moved elsewhere.

In *The Presence of the Actor,* Joseph Chaikin writes, "In ancient Greek theater the actors wore large masks which covered their faces. The crowds were large, and these masks served to represent the main feature of the character wearing them. The characters, for the most part, were portrayed as showing one face to the world, and only in rare cases, such as Oedipus' blinding, was there a second mask for the same character. . . . When the messenger would come onto the stage, he would wear the mask of his over-all response to what he had witnessed. Furthermore, the messenger would carry the news of the significant action, which would never be performed on the stage."

Growing up, we had a white African mask near our front door, its mouth stretched long into the expression of a scream. I can imagine the shouting, looting, angry bodies running around in masks. The expression on all these masks is frozen in the physiognomy of shock, in response to the murder of a young man they have known. The policemen wear masks too, molded into a grimace of a kind of fundamental resolve. The identity of the fighters begins to lose its meaning. The emotions are spare and timeless. It could be a play about some ancient battle that only serves to symbolize to us, these years later, the horrible seduction of hatred, vanity, and power. Emotions as extraordinary as those played out in some Greek myth.

Chaikin writes, of a Polish playwright that he admires, "His work is an articulation of a common human condition. In every moment he seems aware that his 'confession' is something which applies to him but not only to him."

In Aeschylus's Greek tragedy *Agamemnon,* a young girl named Cassandra goes into a trance. At first she sounds crazed, but eventually she reveals that she has been given the ability to see into the future. She asks the chorus what she should do, because she knows that she is about to be murdered with an ax. Anne Carson explains, "Everywhere in Agamemnon there is a leakage of the metaphorical into the literal and the literal into the metaphorical."

In Carson's translation of the play, Cassandra cries, "I am just this sound. I will walk with my song torn open."

Some of the most beloved fans of ska in the 1960s in England were the Hard Mods, and the British skinheads. In fact, according to Les Black's article "Voices of Hate, Sounds of Hybridity," skinhead fashion was an interpretation of Jamaican "rude boy" style: "Ben Shermans, bowling shirts, red or lime green socks and loafers or brogues," in addition to "porkpie hats and too-short Levis." Musical genres like "skinhead reggae" and "northern soul" emerged among skinheads due to an obsession with Jamaican ska and American soul music. A white DJ from that time remembers, "The scene was predominantly working class and the music was and is black American. The dedication and love of the music is incredible. It was addictive—the raw emotion of it. . . . On the dance floor you'll see the 'soul grimace' on their face."

But this did not necessarily mean that the skinheads were especially tolerant of black people. When faced with the notion that "if all blacks left England your music would go with it," a skinhead replied, "We would still have the tapes."

Of the Mods, the playwright Jeff Noon wondered, "I just thought, so what if these young men are creating a beautiful mask for themselves. What happens when you fall out of love with your mask?"

Les Black writes about a black boy traveling with his friend, who was given a "Sieg Heil" from a bunch of footballers. Inside the service station restaurant, a white woman from Liverpool at another table within earshot addressed the entire room: "Will no one here stand up for them?" She and her husband offered to walk them to their car. In this moment, a woman breaks the reality that everyone has come to accept as the norm. She calls attention to the basic humanity that they have forgotten to feel, as though passing smelling salts under the nose of a fainted body.

In the late 1950s, the National Labor Party began to spread its ideology among young working-class white men. They sponsored rallies like "Stop the Coloured Invasion" at Trafalgar Square in 1959, touting the slogan, "Keep Britain White." The Skinheads weren't founded on a principle of racism, but they were encouraged to take it on when politicians suggested that immigrants were the cause of their social disadvantages.

One night in August in 1958, a group of skinheads saw a white woman out with her Jamaican husband. They found her the next night and began to beat her with an iron bar, until the police intervened. Later on, a mob of hundreds of white people went to a house party on Bromley Road, where they began to attack the mostly West Indian residents.

This was not the only racially inspired incident of the time, but it was one of the few wherein policemen actually intervened. The Notting Hill riots began. A recording of the popular ska artist Count Suckle was supposedly playing as the mob descended onto the party on Bromley Road.

In 1981, the year I was born, a racially inspired case of arson in New Cross killed thirteen black teenagers. A member of the British Black Panthers, Darcus Howe, organized a "Black People's March" in protest to the way the case of arson was handled. This protest ended in violence, and not long after the police conducted "Operation Swamp 81," in which officers in plainclothes stopped, searched, and arrested hundreds of people in the heavily black area of Brixton. A young black man died, and many in the community believed that he'd been left to die by the police. Police cars were pelted with bricks. Stores were looted. Fires were started. Stones and bottles. Bottles and bricks.

When I went to London, I wanted to dance to reggae. I asked a friend if I could borrow some Jamaican music. He lent me "Dread Beat an' Blood" by Poet and The Roots, produced by the dub poet Linton Kwesi Johnson. As I walked through the city, I listened to Johnson songs like "The Great Insurrection" on headphones. The YouTube video of this song shows footage of the Brixton riots. Policemen who seem gawky and unsure how to move in their own bodies wear tall, rounded hats. They walk behind long, plastic sheets, grabbing stray rioters and pummeling them with batons. A middle-aged white man passes by a camera with a face of total composure as three young black men behind him set fire to a car. The policemen walk fast or walk slow.

At the time, I felt dragged down by Johnson's monotone, but as I hear it now I hear the voice of a man who is exhausted by the knowledge of his own future, who chooses to sing of it anyway. He was not surprised by the Brixton riots of 1981 any more than Darcus Howe was surprised by those of 2011. In "Man Free," Johnson sings, "Dem can't keep him down, dem can't keep him down, cuz he's a merciless realist. And 'im is not defeatist. And 'im stand up in the court like a mighty lion, 'im stand up in the court like a man of iron." I remember the way Johnson's song curved around the strange name that, at the time I could not recognize: "Darcus out of jail. The people's will must prevail."

During another semester of teaching, I noticed myself feeling anxious. My eyes kept drifting to a student who I'd noticed wearing blue plaid shorts with a pattern that I'd somehow come to associate with skinheads. I started to brew stories in my head until the next week, when he wore a shirt with the same fabric, and I realized that this was more likely a boy who had somehow ended up with a matching blue plaid short suit that his mother picked out at a discount store.

Around the same time, a student expressed discouragement with the way he'd been treated in school. "Most teachers didn't have time for me," he explained, excited to use this as a theme of his first essay. He was clearly very intelligent, and looked a lot, as I think back on it, like the kid in *Parenthood* whose parents are told in a meeting that their son is too much work and ask that he be sent to a special school for children with "emotional problems." Later on, Steve Martin imagines his son standing on a bell tower, shooting into the crowd. But I really liked this kid. He was jovial, made surprisingly sharp references to 1980s R&B music. I enjoyed his presence in class.

In an essay, he made reference to being, among a host of other social roles in high school, a skinhead. Something about this revelation bowled me over, and I raved that it was one of the best essays I'd seen. What I meant was that I felt grateful to him for being so honest with me. He was always kind, so it didn't seem possible to me that he'd retained the ideology of one of the many identities he'd listed.

Not long after, he came to me asking for advice. I was tired at that point in the semester, a little jaded, and less willing to put in extra time to my job. I looked over something he'd been very excited to write and reacted with a kind of bland, rote encouragement that left his face somewhat surprised.

Months later, I was biking to my friend's house, not far from school. A block away from me, a white car full of college-aged boys shot past, and someone leaned his head out the window to shout, "Black bitch!" with such screeching, lingered articulation, it seemed personal. The first face to cross my mind was my old student's. I realize now how quickly I was willing to see us shrink back into our roles: the black teacher and the skinhead. To the masks of self we hold up with such half-assed sincerity.

The work of the Wooster Group is often a way of playing with literal versus metaphorical interpretation. When, years ago, one of their white actors used black face, people who heard about it protested immediately. Critics had a difficult time understanding that it was the loaded cultural symbol of the makeup that they were introducing onto the stage, and not a literal, explicit expression of those associations.

The Wooster Group has used the term *simulacrum* in the title of a play. The *Webster's New Twentieth Century (Unabridged)* dictionary defines this as "1. An image. 2. A mere pretense or semblance; vague representation; counterfeit; travesty; sham."

In a video from 1981, three actors perform the hula. They look more like they are performing swim strokes, and move in profile. They move to the right. They move to the left, rotating their arms in circles. The audience is laughing. How silly they look! How seriously we take ourselves when all we're doing is going through the motions.

In London, I met a woman who had only found out a month before that her father was white. Growing up, everyone pretended that there was no difference between she and her brother, but it was painfully obvious. Her mother was even a bit hostile toward her, having to live with the reminder, perhaps, of a painful relationship. She became annoyed by the social lift afforded to her daughter because she was a tall, light-skinned aberration in the landscape of their African home. Classmates called her "white." Strangers offered them a ride. Salespeople at market offered her a better price. Her mother resented her for it.

"Have you ever had moments where you feel like you've gotten, you've transcended that hostility, or that distance?" I ask her.

She gives me a scenario. "I'm walking down the road, and I see somebody shove somebody else over, for no reason. Like just being blatantly rude or nasty. Just the anger, I walk up to the person and tell them that 'Listen, you can't do that, that's not the right way to behave.' And it's like, really, these are two strangers. It really shouldn't affect you in that way."

But sometimes a private injustice is what helps us to understand the injustice of someone else. The performance of one grief may expunge the pain of another.

In August of 2011, Mark Duggan got shot. He was thought to be a gangster. He ran from the police. They drew. They fired. It happens all the time.

An article in the *Guardian* muses on whether or not he fit the label of a "gangster" or a "father," as if these labels are mutually exclusive: "Hardened north London gangster and drug dealer, or loving family man who would never seek confrontation? Two different portraits were painted of Mark Duggan, the twenty-nine-year-old Tottenham man whose death sparked the weekend's London riots."

Based on interviews and Facebook pages, the article makes a case for Duggan being a gangster. One of the reasons he'd been sought out by police is because his cousin and best friend, Kelvin Easton, had recently been stabbed to death with a broken champagne bottle, and they thought he might be out for revenge. After reading a couple of Greek plays, it's funny to think of revenge as solely within the province of black British "gangsters," but the wording of the article makes it seem that if he was indeed a part of a gang, that would impair readers' ability to sympathize with him or with his family, to understand his grief. "Several shots show him in gangster poses; in others he is dressed in all black, or shown gesturing from behind the wheel of a yellow sportscar with headlights blazing." And yet people somehow had the ability to love him: "I love you like cooked food," reads one comment; "1 thing they can't take is da love I have 4 u two," says another of both Duggan and his deceased best friend.

I imagine my student getting caught up in some crime. Photographs from one of his phases in high school could be used as proof of whatever role they've chosen for him to play. But these narratives have nothing to do with the jokes he had made on the first day of class. The way he felt elated by the notion of a poem. The way he looked when I pretended to read what he had written.

When Joseph Chaikin writes of character, he asks, "Whom do you see when you look at me? Whom do you think I see when I look at you? Who or what is it that you think cannot be seen by anyone — is it still you?"

Joseph Chaikin proposes that the actor complete the following report:

Imagine a burning house:
1. You live in the house that is on fire. Even your clothes are charred as you run from the burning house.
2. You are the neighbor whose house might also have caught fire.
3. You are a passer-by who witnessed the fire by seeing someone who ran from a building while his clothes were still burning.
4. You are a journalist sent to gather information on the house which is burning.
5. You are listening to a report on the radio, which is an account given by the journalist who covered the story of the burning house.

We can place ourselves, for example, in the position of the thirteen teenaged boys who woke up in a house that was on fire in 1981. Even their clothes were charred but they never made it out of the house. We can place ourselves in the position of the neighbor whose house might also have caught fire. We can place ourselves in the position of the boy wearing black boots and a porkpie hat. The strands of a ska tune may have played in his head while a book of matches fell silently from his hand. We could be that reporter. We could be a cop, hiding behind a tall plastic sheet in Los Angeles in 1965, in Brixton in 1981, in Los Angeles in 1992, in Tottenham in 2011.

Chaikin writes, "In effect we are joined to each other (to all living creatures) by what we don't understand."

After Emmet Till's body was mutilated by a group of white men and thrown into the Tallahatchie River with a cotton gin fan tied around his neck, he was given an open-casket funeral. Fred Moten writes of his face, "It was turned inside out, ruptured, exploded, but deeper than that it was opened. As if his face were the truth's condition of possibility, it was opening and revealed." Moten points out that this truth has something to do with the sonic reverberations of the photograph: "One is taken out, as in screams, fainting, tongues, dreams."

At the end of *Blink*, Malcolm Gladwell goes, step by step, through the 1999 police shooting of Guinean immigrant Amadou Diallo in New York City, trying to piece together how it happened that a group of plainclothes cops could have pulled up next to the curb of an unarmed man's apartment, seen him standing on the porch, chased after him, assumed that he was reaching for a gun instead of a wallet, and shot him over and over again. Gladwell points out that in a state of heightened adrenaline or fear, the somewhat inexperienced officers who approached Diallo failed to read the subtle cues in behavior that would have normally communicated to them that he was not a threat. But in a state of what Gladwell describes as "temporary autism," the expressions of innocence, curiosity, and fear on Diallo's face and body were not read. So the cops filled him in with their subconscious assumptions of what a black man standing on a porch late at night in a bad neighborhood *could* mean, has meant, in movies, on the news, through actors, through broadcasters, in the scripts we have written and performed. Then they filled him with forty-one shots. When he saw that the black object in Diallo's hand was a wallet and not a gun, one of the officers crouched down next to the dying body and began to cry.

On an online memorial, Mark Duggan's godmother writes, "R.i.p. Mark darling may god bless u and Kelvin and keep u both safe. now ive lost 2 sons. please no more i beg u. r.i.p. my sons."

The dictionary of Caribbean English usage that I've checked out from the library is a poetic tome of words and phrases taken from islands such as Jamaica, St. Lucia, Tobago, Belize, and Trinidad as well as Britain and America. The verb *cry* is translated as "cry longwater (out of your eye). Cry big water. Cry bucket-a-drop. Cry burying cry. Cry living eye water."

So many people complained about his treatment after his interview that Darcus Howe was issued an apology from the BBC. And what I think people meant when they called on the reporter's rudeness was that she'd committed a faux pas at a funeral. When the mourners pass, you remove your hat. You remove your mask. You bow your head toward the loss and you feel it. When the woman in the blazer stopped Howe from speaking about the death of Mark Duggan, she was silencing Cassandra, who has only a grieving howl to sing in the face of her own destruction. As she wrapped up the broadcast, she was hesitant to lift her eyes to the camera. I wonder if she realized that in the act of doing her job, she had held up her hands like an objection or a shield in the face of her own catharsis.

Paris, France

Resolution in Bearing

"Last night at dinner, Sarah asked me if I was close to my father," my dad says. I am in Tucson, in a house that smells faintly of sewage, surrounded by pomegranate trees with rust-colored fruit and hundred-degree heat. Monsoon season has started and the afternoon sky is dark gray with clouds. My father is in our Los Angeles apartment, surrounded by my mother's orchids, snaking succulents, jade plants, and rosemary. This is the first day my phone has worked since I returned home from Portugal, and he is catching me up on what I've missed, namely a dinner party with old friends. "I told her that when I was little, my father would smell me. I did the same thing with you." When my dad starts to talk about his father I feel heavy and a little spun. So I sit on the couch with the phone on my belly in speaker mode, as though we are in the room together.

"When you were a baby you had a fragrance that I grew accustomed to. I could find you in the dark." I think of the Polaroid photographs of my father, muscular and shirtless with unkempt hair and a wild beard, holding a premature, jaundiced infant in the palm of his hand. I try, too, to imagine my grandfather in a similar pose, holding my dad, though the effort to conjure my own father as an infant pushes me too far. Infancy and death are, perhaps, too similar, and I don't like imagining him so vulnerable. "If I carry it a step further," he continues, "I could find you beyond the grave." I know that death is on my father's mind. It always is. He is a hypochondriac, so I've learned to brush off his morbid moments. But it's harder to feel at a remove when I see how the notion of his own death slaps him in the face every time an old friend dies. I encourage him to do yoga in the hopes that some teacher will coach him to keep his mind on the present instead of lurking in the halls of an imagined afterlife.

The apartment was spare when I was born, with a brown carpet instead of the gray it is now. There was no bookcase with a thousand books, no stereo, no red velvet couch cover or African masks, no embroidered pillowcases from Pretoria, no glass table, no stack of art books, not much furniture at all. I imagine him navigating the space of our apartment in 1981 in the dark, where there was so much less chance of stubbing your toe, following my scent to the crib. "When you were a baby, I told your mom, 'If I should die early, put something in the casket that smells like her.'"

Not long ago, my parents both wore sweaters for a day before sending them to me in the mail so that I could feel closer to them, which struck me as extreme. But both of them have lost parents and know what it is to mourn something as simple as scent. This moves me more now, as my father and I have been distant lately. A series of fights during a road trip about a year ago have made things between us oddly fragile. Even though we talk often, every time we are on the phone feels like the first time we've spoken since our fight. This conversation is, by far, the most tender we've had in a long time. I don't know what it will take to make the air between us lighten. A moment like this calls attention to our waiting, though, like the pending storm outside, for the time when the relationship will be released into a new state of being, and we can be present together.

"When I was little, my father was doing the same thing with me. He pulled me to him, I realize, because he wanted to smell me. He would bounce me on his knee and sing a song in a language I couldn't understand." My father speaks with an air of pride when he refers to my grandfather's time in Europe during the war. This is where, I assume, he picked up this song, which my father begins to sing, reconstituting the foreign sounds phonetically. "Buntum baby" he sings and repeats, energized by the memory of his father's voice.

When I was sixteen, I spent New Year's Eve in the living room of our apartment. I had strewn blankets on the floor, and my mom dozed on the couch, sleepy from the small glass of Grand Marnier that I'd poured for her. My father must have been traveling. On the television, home videos from our family vacations were playing. I sat on the floor with legs crossed as my mother snored, watching our family move through a set of familiar scenes.

My mother had often complained during our family vacations because my father was always squinting behind the foot-long, news-quality camcorder that he held on his shoulder. He would film the woman at the café talking to the customer, in close-up and then from the mirrored ceiling; the poster advertising an upcoming visit from the Dalai Lama as a moped zooms by on a nearby street; the woman who can't keep her eyes off of the young, interracial couple on the Paris metro. But too, there is his young white wife, smiling to her mother while she holds the brown baby on her hip as they wait for the train to Rome.

I've seen so much of my childhood through the veneer of muted tones, heaviest in dust yellow and cyan. I know just how to replicate this balance of color in Photoshop and often find myself on the computer fixing the pictures I take to match the faded quality of my father's videos. Once he overlaid a track of horribly cheesy R&B onto footage of patrons at the Picasso museum in Paris. Men and women wearing shoulder pads and permed hair weave among each other or stand in contemplation of the self-portraits and cubist bulls while a deep-voiced singer sings and the electronic imitation of a bubble bursting plays over the ambient sound. My father's home videos make the past into an easily re-entered moment. Because there isn't much plot, the scenes are like landscapes that can be walked into and inhabited. You can join the woman at the café bar, sit in front of a wall-sized Picasso, or stay on the train watching the couple, because this is where they live.

Wim Wenders captures that quality of time. His orientation toward quiet, subtle moments creates a space for the viewer to enter into the scene more than is often the case in feature films. In an interview for *DoubleTake*, he says, "My first films were basically landscape paintings, except that they were shot with a movie camera. I never moved the frame." His first long film was about a man who gets out of prison: "Nothing much happens except that he listens to a lot of music and drives around the city, so content to be at liberty again." So it is that we come to feel so much for his characters. We've sat with them for so long as they exist before the camera that we forget that time, location, or a screen separates us from one another. Or we become them.

In the film *Paris, Texas*, Wenders tells the story of a man who comes out of the desert with a plastic gallon jug of water in his hand. He has been missing for four years, and when his brother finds him, he drives him home to Los Angeles. The man who stumbled out of the desert hardly remembers his past. He sits in the living room of his brother's home as his tow-headed son watches him shyly. Home movies from the life he left play, projected on the wall in front of him. Eventually, he starts to remember. The footage in these videos is some of the most beautiful in the entire film: a smiling woman playing with her husband's moustache, a little boy gazing below the dock, the blue-toned shot of a seagull passing. It is as though Wenders sets the home movie up as an ideal that his own film hopes to replicate. It introduces the depth of emotion that, if his own slowly rendered story does its job correctly, we will experience again once we come close enough to the characters.

At the end, the man finds his estranged wife working at a peep-show club in Austin. He tells her the story of their lives through the half-silvered glass of a one-way mirror. She gazes into her own reflection, listening to a story about a woman who "dreamed of running naked down the highway, running across fields, running down river-beds, always running." The man ties a cowbell around the woman's ankle so that he can hear if she runs away. He ties her to the oven. At first she is sweet and a little chirpy, but she begins to cry when she knows the story to be her own. This is the payoff of Wenders's style of filmmaking, because we too will realize, once we stare long enough at the man who "ran from a fire until every sign of man had disappeared," that we are looking at ourselves.

My father's home videos have the attributes of a realist work. B-roll footage collaged together with captured moments from our lives create a kind of art film. The Italian neorealist Vittorio De Sica and the French filmmaker Eric Rhomer have both made movies as simply, with such casual dialogue, assembling plot from the pose of non-actors who are engaged in almost real life in front of a camera. Vittorio De Sica believed that everyone could play one role perfectly: himself. So when I started to watch our home movies as a teenager, after watching hours of independent and foreign film on cable television, I started to invest in the story that the film created as though it lived both through and outside of myself. I saw it with just enough temporal remove to have to wonder at emotions and uncaptured dialogue. I could encounter my own life as art, with the objective mind-set of a film viewer, and when I had the filmgoer's moment of epiphany—of identification with the characters—the poetry of the moment was incalculably strong.

A while ago, I picked a book off of my father's shelf: *The Film Sense*, by Sergei Eisenstein. Writes Eisenstein, "The lifelike acting of an actor is built, not on his representing the copied results of feelings, but on his causing the feelings to *arise, develop, grow into other feelings*—*to live before the spectator*" (emphasis original). He also writes, "A work of art, understood dynamically, is just this process of arranging images in the feelings and mind of the spectator."

My early appreciation for what film could evoke in me through my father's subtly produced home videos has made me especially attracted to the film work of artists who focus less on plot and more on quiet, observed being. Directors of this kind are exactly poets, who present only the slivered down haiku of a story, which in its Buddhist simplicity resounds like a vibration.

During the summer of my sixteenth year, I boarded an airplane with my father. In a giant journal that I'd made from cardboard, gray suede, and binder clips, I wrote about my inability to feel the present moment. I was obsessed with Oscar Wilde and had spent a good amount of time weeping over *De Profundis*, the letter written while Wilde was in prison for gross indecency. In it, he writes, "The Mystical in Art, the Mystical in Life, the Mystical in Nature this is what I am looking for. It is absolutely necessary for me to find it somewhere." I had also read *Mrs. Dalloway* for school. Fifteen pages in, I felt as though someone had redefined the world for me. The unifying nature of Woolf's language, tying together every character it touched, felt like a call to some kind of compassionate, creative action that I was clueless as to how to enact. But I was also a hormonal teenager and spent most of my time feeling impatient and grouchy.

While we flew, I became confused. When was it going to feel real that we were leaving the country? I had spent weeks assembling a wardrobe of clothes that I'd never worn before, many of them snatched from my mother's closet. I was, at the time, in an Annie Hall phase of dressing, and had chopped off all of my hair. This trip was an experiment in some new self. I took a photograph of the silhouette of a cute boy across the aisle, who was also writing in his journal.

I made eyes with an attractive woman, who reminded me of a girl I had a crush on in school. I was straining to be a new person, in the wardrobe of an earlier time. Paris would somehow act as a time machine, bringing to life the adult persona I craved to inhabit: a funky, biracial fusion of my mother and Diane Keaton, taking to the streets of the circa-1980s Paris I'd been watching in our home videos. Joni Mitchell and Bob Dylan played on the mixtape my friend had made for me, exaggerating the degree to which my vision of the future was overlaid by nostalgia for the past.

Meanwhile, beside me, my father held images in his head of the men who'd taken this journey before him. Years back, he'd spent long hours in the company of a cartoonist named Ollie Harrington, who told him stories of the friendship he shared with Richard Wright and Chester Himes in Paris. The trio would sit at the Café Trounon over green aperitifs, jotting down notes, gossiping and laughing loudly as people walked past the newsstand at a gate of the Luxembourg Gardens. An elegant man who is often complimented for his many fedoras, my father sat with his camera at his feet, an open book on the tray table in front of him, jotting down ideas in the margins for the next project he'd embark upon.

At the arrival gate, we drank espresso and ate croissants, mystified by the fact that people were smoking inside. I shot pictures of the rental car kiosk, of my father on a pay phone, of men and women standing in front of the smooth surfaces of the airport's wall and floors.

I rode with my father in an Avis rental car to a café called Le Royale. We slammed the doors. They locked. I looked inside to see keys swinging from the ignition. I spent my first hour in Paris banished to a café by my father, crying like a five-year-old, ignoring the espresso shot delivered to me, waiting for a young North African man to jimmy the lock to our sedan. Eventually, we were in the car again. We made it to the place where we were staying, and sooner or later, sleep arrived. I awoke at three o'clock in the morning on a small cot, terrified. The bathroom walls were ornate pink tile and the small apartment was lined with shelves full of photographs from all over the world. My father was sleeping on the floor. We both got up, despite the hour, and made tea. I discovered that writing in my journal made the terror of the unfamiliar die down. I wrote, "It's a record, a clamping down on time."

He'd buy a gyro in the Latin Quarter, and I'd eat his greasy french fries. We spent time with expats in a Chinese restaurant, where a thin woman who seemed as though she might disappear asked a young Finnish poet to read his work without translating, to see if we could intuit the meaning. During the summer when we lived in Paris, I shifted between feeling lonely, angry, or close with my father. I wrote often of missing him "already." I complained of feeling too conscious of the future and of death. Being stranded with him in a foreign place drew my attention to his mortality.

We were staying, for a couple of days, in the office of a photojournalist friend of my father's. After the photojournalist and his family left for the summer, my father and I would be able to move into their apartment, four floors up and radiant in vibrant fabrics, handcrafted wooden toys, books, and professional family photographs curated like an exhibit. The wife was Dutch, blonde, breathtakingly beautiful, and much taller than I'd expected. She asked if I wanted to go shopping. The husband spoke rocket fast, had a comedian for a brother, and had curly brown hair. They spoke three languages with their son, whose name sounds like an African stone, and their daughter was just a baby. I was struck by how much I adored them in the short time we spent together. I remember us all going to a party. I felt suddenly aware of a new way that my body occupied space, walking as I did inside the slow, flat pace of travel where every second of the present moment lasts for a hundred years. We walked home and I dribbled a basketball down the cobblestones with an eight-year-old who looked, a bit, like the little boy from *Paris, Texas*. Once they left, my father and I would spend our evenings filming the spectators at Hotel de Ville, as they watched the World Cup match on giant screens. Men perched like birds on streetlamps. The neon glow of a Chinese restaurant made for a nice contrast with the blue-toned dusk and taxis.

Many days were spent at the Shakespeare & Company bookstore, on the second floor, where my father interviewed an eccentric Australian woman named Mary Louise for a radio story he was writing. She painted Shakespeare's face in puffy paint onto black tee shirts while speaking in long monologues about raising her children with her mother in a tent outside of Rome. I scratched at the real or imagined bedbugs attacking my backside, sketching a profile of Oscar Wilde's mother in ballpoint pen onto the cover of my journal, not so secretly blushing over the Salvador Dalí lookalike silhouetted by the window who didn't know I existed as he sipped tea from a stained cup. To save money on food, we would go to the market for rotisserie chicken and cheese. Or I would go to a supermarket and vegetable stand to practice my French. I made soup or pasta for lunch. For the first time in my life, cooking was not something that I was doing to help my mother in the kitchen. I had a role, and because it was temporary and more adult than I was used to, it gave me great pleasure. I was surprised at how fresh the vegetables were, each meal a small masterpiece of flavor when cooked with just a bit of salt, garlic, and oil.

One Sunday, we rose at six o'clock in the morning. We walked to the yet-to-open museums and took pictures of graffiti. We window-shopped at unopened stores and enjoyed a Paris devoid of many other people. We got bread, then I took a nap. Later that day, I wore black linen pants and a red sweater. As I read these details in my old diary, a pipeline of juxtaposed images starts to flicker, as though pieces of film are standing side by side on a light box. I can feel the buzz of what I've forgotten just beyond my grasp. The act of not quite remembering is not unlike the act of listening to the spare poetry of Wim Wenders's dialogue: "Here we are in the Mojave Desert in a place that doesn't have a name," one man says to his brother.

A young Frenchwoman assisted in the production of *Paris, Texas*. Claire Denis is white and blonde and grew up in Africa, following her parents to the places where her father worked as a civil servant, like Burkina Faso, Somalia, Senegal, and Cameroon. Many of her films take place in Africa or portray immigrant populations in a European setting.

Often, her characters are shown at two different periods of their lives, so that, as Ruth Watson writes, "Two distinct historical periods are fused into an eternal present and Denis constructs the 'timeless air of the nostalgia film.'" Such a style is doubly nostalgic for me, because Denis's quiet, observing lens calls to mind my father's films. Like my father's long shots of strangers, her camera gazes, stares like an idle people watcher who happens to notice a stranger in a moment when she doesn't realize she's being seen. Watson says of a character caught onscreen in Denis's film, *Chocolat*, "We see her discomfort as she fidgets and curls her toes inwards. But perhaps we should not overinterpret her body language. Maybe she behaves this way because she finds the concrete on which she stands too hot for her tender bare feet. Such ambiguity is characteristic of Claire Denis's *Chocolat*." Nostalgia is even more compounded for we children of the eighties because that is the "present" of Denis's work.

Denis says in an interview, "A lot of people came from the French Caribbean to work on the railways in the 1960s. I was listening to the radio and they were interviewing drivers. One guy was interesting: he was explaining the pull of the track and how the concentration was such an introspective thing. He said it was the kind of job that leads you to knowing yourself quite well." One of her more recent films, *35 Shots of Rum*, centers around a subway train driver of Caribbean origin living outside of Paris with his biracial daughter. When I saw the film, I was unable to speak about it after it was over. I rarely see characters who so closely resemble my own family, and I felt as though I'd been dreaming a memory. Even when her characters aren't living during the 1980s, her films often look as though they are. I can't say that she goes through an editing process like I do to get my photographs to resemble my father's Kodachrome prints, but some quality in even her recent work connotes that era. In this way, as I watch, I feel as though I'm seeing different versions of my own family history. A train conductor who could be my father but in a different country with a different job, history, and cultural role. A taxi driver from the Caribbean sips at a cup of soup from a thermos, her door opening out on the chilly afternoon. Calypso flows out of her car like steam.

In the beginning of the film, a black man named Lionel stands on an outdoor train platform and smokes a cigarette. In a shot that will repeat throughout the film, we can see the tracks stretch out before us, catching light. Lionel's daughter, Josephine, holds the pole in a subway car, perhaps the one her father is driving. When she returns home to an empty apartment, she begins peeling garlic for dinner. She greets Lionel when he arrives with a kiss on the cheek and brings him his slippers. He bathes as she finishes making dinner. The camera begins to take in the environment around this small family: a young man trips going up the dark stairwell of the building. A woman smokes out the window. The yellow-, green-, and blue-toned squares of light that constitute an apartment complex glow like tiny TV screens.

Denis based *35 Shots of Rum* in part on her own family. "I was raised with this story of the perfect father, my grandfather. My mother would tell us she was sad because, although she was married with children, she missed her father."

When I was younger, my mother and I took a walk one afternoon to the end of our street, and in turning the corner passed a house with high walls. Ivy grew along the outside and delicate white flowers hung around the entry to the gate. I can't remember if there was a party going on inside, but I was so reminded by it of the garden parties my parents took me to as a child that I felt we'd entered back into the past. I began walking this route often, peering between the wrought-iron rungs to glimpse the scene from my childhood that I was convinced played out on the other side.

When my father worked as a photojournalist, we went to these kinds of parties often, in the San Fernando Valley, Malibu, and Hollywood. I see films like Henry Jaglom's *Eating*, where women with perms are dressed in big blazers, gossiping around a pool in Hancock Park, and add myself: a three-year-old curly haired nut with little interest in adult conversation, zigzagging between the lawn chairs. During one of these parties, my father was standing with a group of people, several cameras hanging around his neck. When he heard a splash and could see from someone's expression that I'd fallen into the pool, he took two steps, cameras swinging, and plunged into the water to retrieve me. For a photographer who can recount every ounce of equipment he has lost or had stolen with perfect clarity, this sacrifice has become a kind of familial myth, a song of his ferocious loyalty.

When I was about three years old, my parents watched as I boarded a carousel in Paris and found a horse to ride. There weren't many other children around. It should have been a quaint scene. "You should have seen him," my mom recalls, laughing. My father saw a man walking toward me and bounded onto the carousel to accost him. My mother was unable to break through the action adventure plot he was now starring in. "He's the ticket collector!" she screamed. "That poor man," my mother says of the innocent carousel employee as she recounts the story to me now. "He must have been terrified."

Through its language of blue and yellow, *35 Shots of Rum* reminds me of Shakespeare's *Tempest*, another father-daughter tale. In this version, a man trying to learn how to harness the power of nature raises his daughter on an island, surrounded by magical spirits. In a film version of the story starring Molly Ringwald, a man stands at the window of his high-rise, summoning a thunderstorm. It seems we're supposed to be noticing Prospero's vanity as he attempts to harness the power of the natural world for his own benefit. But in the context of a father raising his daughter, I see him in a different light. Was it hubris that caused the man to test his power over the weather? Or a wish to rock the world to sense for the sake of his daughter?

In *35 Shots of Rum*, Josephine's mother was a German woman who was, before she died, terrified of the ocean. One day, gazing at the tracks before him, Lionel imagines riding on a black horse with his child. Denis explains that this image comes from a German song that she imagines Lionel would have known, Schubert's "Der Erlkonig." It is a song about a father trying to care for his sick child. "It's a poem. It's like a prayer. Oh, my child, my *kind*, please don't die. It's full of fear and anxiety of . . ." the director trails off.

Josephine and Lionel go to Germany together in an old van. Sleeping on the beach, near that entity of which the missing wife and mother felt so afraid, Josephine tells her father: "I wish we could stay like this forever." This makes those of us watching feel ill at ease. We know there's something unsustainable about this kind of grasping. Father and daughter cannot live together forever. At some point they will need to let go. Holding her hands in his own one day, he tells her, "Feel free."

One of the reasons that my father and I had journeyed to France is so that I could take language lessons at the Alliance Française. I awoke in the top bunk of a bed on the first day of school with the worst cramps I'd ever experienced. The piercing I'd gotten in the cartilage of my right ear was feeling infected and I was homesick. One thing fathers and husbands seem to have been protected from, in my understanding, is the way that the word *cramps* is a euphemism for things like explosive diarrhea.

After he convinced me that staying home was not an option, I did what I could, without an ibuprofen in sight, to prepare for school, complaining that there were not enough pads or tampons to last me through the day. My father practically jogged in place, so eager was he to start our journey. "Let's go!" he shouted merrily through the bathroom door. "We'll stop at a pharmacy on the way there." I hobbled alongside him on what felt to be the longest walk of my life, which my memory sees as a nauseous compilation of faces, dog shit, cobblestones, and storefronts. We searched for an electric green cross signifying the closest pharmacy where we could buy the necessary items. We skipped coffee and a croissant that day, and instead he handed me a cup of hot tea. We cut across the Luxembourg Gardens, eventually making our way to Boulevard Raspail. "See you after class!" he said jovially as he waved to me from the front door of the school. Throughout the course of that summer, we sent faxes back and forth to my mother, who tried to offer the necessary translation that would help my father and I make sense to one another.

The walk to school became, eventually, a ritual. My father took great pleasure in seeing me transform from a sleepy, grouchy teenager to, after a coffee and croissant, a chatty, jogging woman. In reading my diary from that time, I discover something I hadn't remembered. Oftentimes, during these walks, my father held my hand, as though I were a little girl.

The French won the World Cup that summer. That night, the streets were on fire with tiny red and blue explosions, and ecstatic bodies were suddenly everywhere. We descended into a metro station so that we could film people at the Champs Elysées, and in his hurried pace through the thick crowds of people, my father grasped at the hand of the person walking behind him on an electronic people mover between platforms. A young man shouted and yanked his hand away, swearing at my father as he pushed beyond him. I watched cheerfully as my father realized his mistake. I grabbed onto his hand and made fun of him for years.

Upon hearing about my father's hypochondria, a woman in my meditation group tells me, "Masculine energy is all about emptiness, which, with the right spiritual guidance, can lead you to a kind of Buddhist mentality. But our culture does the opposite. It draws their attention to war, to death." On another day, a man talks about trying to reach out to the daughter of his deceased friend. Apparently, she has been posting messages to her dead father on his Facebook page. A question forms in my head. "What would you tell her?" And tears start to seep onto my face as if from a tepid faucet. The emotion feels exquisite, like an answer to the question I've had about my father for so long: why can't I stand to talk to him? Why do I feel impatient on the phone? My mother tells me that I have always had the habit of distancing myself from people when I fear they are about to leave.

In *The Tempest*, father and daughter puzzle over the idea of origin, peering inside one another's perceptions of the past. Miranda doesn't know much about how they've ended up on the island, and she tells her father: "You have often begun to tell me what I am, but stopped and left me to a bootless inquisition Concluding, *Stay not yet.*" Prospero asks, "What seest thou else in the dark backward and abysm of time?" As I think of these lines, now, I wonder if he is asking about her memory of childhood, or if what Prospero is asking from his daughter is more abstract than that. Does he want to know if she remembers her own birth? Perhaps he wants to know what his own future will look like, gazing as he is toward his own death. His child acts as a kind of seer. ("I never thought you were dead," the little boy in *Paris, Texas* says to his father. "I could always feel you walking and talking.")

Ultimately, Prospero recognizes that he will need to encourage his daughter to marry, though the notion gives him great pain.

When their car stalls in a rain shower one night, Lionel, Josephine, and two neighbors take shelter in an African woman's bar. The music starts to play, and father and daughter dance. Soon, though, a young male friend cuts in, and the father steps away, as though realizing for the first time that this is the future that his life will hold: a separation from his child. He responds by flirting with the beautiful proprietress. Meanwhile, the Commodores are singing "Night Shift," an elegy for Marvin Gaye and Jackie Wilson, R&B musicians who both died in 1984. The song acts as a kind of lullaby for the men, as though death were an unfamiliar forest or back alley: "Gonna be a long night, it's gonna be alright, on the nightshift." The song's emotionality comes from the deep sense of hope that the singers, in their blue leather pants and shoulder pads, have as they guide Marvin and Jackie gently into the afterlife.

The song is, if listened to at more of a remove, a kind of shout-out to those folks who are scheduled to work at a time or a place that makes them feel alienated from the rest of the world. "Night shift" is an apt enough way of describing Lionel's job driving the train, as much of his time is spent underground, in darkness. In this way, his job seems a kind of metaphor for the inevitable end of his tunnel. One day, he pulls the train to a stop because his headlights have fallen onto the body of a man. His navigation through darkness acts, perhaps, as a reminder that, while death is surely where Lionel is heading, he cannot responsibly take his daughter with him.

I wonder whether the entire film is a ghost story. Whether or not the whole cast of characters are actually, in that wintry Parisian gloom, already dead, or at least, asleep within the deadened emotions of an inhumane social system. Students at Josephine's school protest because the administration is trying to get rid of the anthropology department, as if to verify the sense that these brown bodies wandering through the chilly streets are meant to remain invisible. At one point, a fellow student quotes Franz Fanon: "We revolt because for whatever reason, we can no longer breathe." The Eiffel Tower–less version of Paris depicted by Denis's camera seems ripe for, as Patricia Falguieres writes, "scenes of recovery, of coming out of a stupor, of waking to one's own stupor — the stupor of history equal to the stupor of animals." Perhaps Josephine is being encouraged to seek a different fate than that of her father. He's hoping she'll find her way out of Hades.

I spent most of my time that summer dreaming. Sometimes literally. My father encouraged me to spend a few hours in the basement language lab after class, and I would fall asleep listening to an energetic narrator reading *Le Petit Prince* through a pair of massive rented headphones. I always faded into sleep around the time when the prince asks his new friend to draw him a sheep. One of my classmates was a short Colombian man named George. "He would have slayed a dragon for you," my father remembers, "but he couldn't have been more invisible to you."

Toward the end of the summer, my mother came to join us, around the same time that the Dutch relatives of our host came to spend a couple of weeks in Paris. Instead of appreciating the overtures of kind, attentive George, I stared over my Kir Royal at their son, who flirted with me just enough to keep me hoping. My journal entries from that time are a manic attempt to recall every moment of interaction between us, interspersed with sad affirmations of the fact that he was not actually interested in me. I took a photograph of him, lying shirtless on the bed of our host's beautiful apartment, a sarcastic Adonis who seemed quite content to bask in my affection. "I could have killed him," my father remembers. "I don't know if it was first love, but it was very difficult for me. And mom would say this is part of growing up, but on my end it was sort of like, it was strange. In a number of ways it was like, a period when you were sort of moving away. It was a season where you were coming of age, the young woman was blossoming."

"What do you remember most about that summer?" I ask. He doesn't skip a beat. "The walks to school. It was a ritual that we took together. On the one hand I was aware that you wanted to be free of me, but on the other hand, it was something we did together. Sometimes we would stop at that restaurant at the base of the park, and sometimes you would just leave and walk the rest of the way by yourself. I think we reached a point where you'd say, *OK dad, I'm cool from here, see ya.*" I continued along, muttering *dessine-moi un mouton*, gaping at the cherry blossoms, dodging the anachronistic-seeming African man dressed in all white who waved to me almost every week from a distance.

Claire Denis was inspired to make *35 Shots of Rum* because of a film by Yasujiro Ozu. In *Late Spring*, a widower lives with his adult daughter, Noriko, in postwar Japan. Worried that she'll never marry so long as he's alone, he pretends that he is engaged in order to trick her into leaving home to marry.

As I watch each cheerful black-and-white scene, I am aware that I feel a sense of struggle to endure the film. I am heavy with a feeling of sad anticipation for the time when the daughter will wed and depart. Each moment the two of them spend together makes the thought of their separation more difficult to bear. "It's pointless to have a daughter," the father tells his friend. "You raise them and off they go. If they don't marry, you worry. If they do marry, you feel let down."

One day, father and daughter visit a Noh play. This form of theater often involves little rehearsal, embodying the spirit of passing time and chance encounter. The men on stage sing a song that brings the spring blossoms outside the theater onto the stage, emphasizing the fragile beauty of the day.

> this is the hedge planted
> next to our old home
> only the color remains
> as it was back then
> only the color remains
> as it was back then
> the color carries with it
> the name of that man from long ago

While the play seems as though it wants to evoke a romantic story, the fact that it sits in the center of a film about a father and a daughter orients the song toward a new pairing: the masked man on stage who impersonates a woman singing with nostalgia becomes Noriko, and the man from long ago becomes her fondly remembered father.

> the scent of wild orange flowers mingles together
> with the sprig of blue flag in his hair
> iris and blue flag so much alike
> whose color is deeper?

During the song, the father nods his head at the woman who he has tricked his daughter into thinking he plans to marry. As the music continues, Noriko lowers her head, overwhelmed with what seems to be a sense of loss for the man beside her. I become impatient with her character after a while, frustrated with her resistance to change.

As they leave the theater, Noriko tells her father that she has something to do and hurries quickly to walk in front of him. And it is in this configuration that I realize my own impatience stems from the character's limbo. Noriko can't escape the waiting either, and she doesn't want to. When she tells her father that she doesn't want to leave, he tells her that his own life is nearing its end. Her new life is just beginning. "That's the order of human life and history," he explains, shooing her back to youth.

On a visit to the Kodai Temple in Kyoto, father and daughter sleep on mats on the floor. Noriko is still speaking to her father when she realizes that he is asleep, or pretending to be. Her gaze shifts to the shadow of trees through the paper window. At some point, she will marry. Her father will return home alone and cut the skin off of an apple with his knife, letting a single peel fall to the floor before he bows his head.

Michael Atkinson writes of Ozu's style, "It just so happens that Ozu's Zen-infused sensibility translates on film to something like the art form's nascent formal beauty: patiently watching little happen, and the meditative moments around the nonhappening, until it be comes crashingly apparent that lives are at stake and the whole world is struggling to be reborn."

I have a photograph of Marvin Gaye on my kitchen wall. My father took it before Gaye was shot by his father in 1984. When I first saw the print, I shrieked with delight, which makes me laugh now because I didn't even realize who it was. I was just so taken with the photograph's intimacy and detail. Gaye is in profile, his unkempt hair twists together in places, a small hoop earring hangs on his left ear while he is looking down. His hand gathers in a loose fist above the detailed texture of his shirt collar and overalls. My dad took the picture at some point during the same day that, through a cloud of marijuana smoke, Gaye sang some of the songs from the album *Let's Get It On* in private concert.

Toward the end of our difficult road trip last summer, my father and I stopped at a gas station and took pictures of each other against a radiant blue sky, in front of a spilled puddle of thick yellow paint that we'd discovered at the edge of the parking lot. I can't remember what city we were in, but beyond the pavement the land turned into a cactus-studded desert. In the car, I put on a Marvin Gaye album. As we listened to "If I Should Die Tonight," my father spoke about the high notes that Gaye kept reaching and shook his head with pleasure. I tried as hard as I could to keep my mind from crawling forward to the day I'd hear the song in a future without him. But it was a strain to keep still, to simply listen to the music alongside him as he hummed.

Brooklyn, New York

White Space

More African American men are in prison or jail, on probation or parole than were enslaved in 1850, before the Civil War began.
—*Michelle Alexander (2011)*

One summer, not long after I graduated from college, I was an anxious wreck. I had just moved to New York City by myself and lived for a while in a family friend's apartment on the Lower East Side. I let the tea kettle burn on the stove, began to drink beer at dusk medicinally, and stood in the hallway, squinting into darkness in the middle of the night, trying not to lose it while my best friend told me over the phone about the ghosts she'd seen while dozing at a bar in Montana. Walking around helped, but never on the weekends. Errands run on Saturdays ensured a series of panic attacks inspired by the thick ocean of pedestrians surrounding me on the as yet unfamiliar streets. One day, I put in an application at a big chain bookstore and got a job in the café. It was easiest to breathe when, after the store closed at midnight, I could walk home through Astor Place toward the Lower East Side as the city cooled.

In search of familiarity, I bought a CD by Paul Simon: *Songs from the Cape Man,* the soundtrack to the Paul Simon and Derek Walcott musical about a Puerto Rican man named Salvador Agron who killed two teenagers in 1959. The musical failed miserably. But the melodies were catching. I fell in love with the album despite the outrageously hokey nature of the songs, perhaps because it was the only CD I had. Just as I was, in that period, hazily grafting together images of the city as I walked it early in the morning and late at night, the lyrics knit together scenes of the city I was learning to inhabit. Together, Simon and I sang, a funky duo of revelers, crooning our love for a complicated city that we longed to see through pastel-colored glasses.

Tiffany was my coworker in the café. She was younger than I was, of Dominican origin, had coffee with cream skin, and lived in Washington Heights. She was in her early twenties and spoke lovingly of her one-year-old son. I listened to her talk about her son and covered for her while she texted her mother in the back room during slow periods in the day. Meanwhile, on my walks home, Paul Simon sang of the kind of neighborhood I imagined she returned to at night, conjuring for me a picture of her home life that must have been about as accurate as the set of *Sesame Street*: "Oh-woh-oh, Carlos and Yolanda dancing in the hallway." We looked quite similar and couldn't have been more different, and this fascinated me.

There wasn't much to do at the café. A nice guy with a long braid down his back named Anthony checked in on us periodically, but there wasn't much to fail at. We met our duties without much effort, and the customers were happy. I felt self-conscious about my background there, as most of my coworkers were single mothers who lived in Washington Heights, while I was a student living alone with hardly any responsibilities beyond feeding myself. I asked them question after question about their children and their boyfriends, and I began to feel mild disdain for the people who worked on the floor of the bookstore, wearing their English degrees like capes when they came to ask for discounted coffees without making an effort to learn our names. My own English degree stayed easily hidden behind my skin, and I liked it there. I never made an attempt to strike up conversation with the booksellers out of irritation with the smug way they cascaded through their position in the store's hierarchy without seeming to question it. So long as I didn't open my mouth to reveal my private-schooled California tongue, I was able to blend in with the tonal range of brown skins behind the counter. Only my immediate coworkers were privy to the fact that I was, most certainly, an alien in their midst.

Born in New York City in 1948, Adrian Piper became the first tenured African American woman in the field of philosophy. She is also a conceptual artist. While in graduate school, she began to read the philosophical writings of Immanuel Kant. Passages from *Critique of Pure Reason* so riveted her that she needed to take breaks from reading it to go look at herself in the mirror to make sure she still existed.

When a cute young blonde woman from Colorado was hired to manage the café, I was immediately suspicious. I was not aware that we needed much more management than what Anthony offered. We suffered through her unnecessary directives, moving things around so that she could feel as though she were fulfilling her duty to impose order. But it felt that, without even her own knowledge, her presence was a mere concession to the customers. A sign that someone was in charge in the way we have come to accept without question: someone white. The first thing she did, besides having us move a display of tea canisters over a few inches to the left, was to catch Tiffany texting and to, with relief that she could finally exercise her burden of power, fire her.

After a while, I moved to Brooklyn. I interviewed at a small gallery near my apartment. The man who hired me was a small, round-faced Puerto Rican designer who had come to some renown in the eighties art scene. He trusted me to edit his e-mails. While he spoke with grace of the aesthetic history of this and that, and laughed about the raucous times he'd spent with people whose names were written on the spines of books on his well-organized shelves, his grammar was spotty and he reminded me of Mrs. Malaprop. Every now and then he'd get a call from his mother, and it was only then that he would speak in Spanish, quietly, quickly, with a harried whisper. She raised him in Spanish Harlem, and he spoke of her with kindness. He was rich now, rubbed scuffs from his shoes and straightened his tie. He made clever lamps that appeared on *Sex in the City* and in hotels around the world. He looked to Rilke for guidance and spoke quotes about Buddhism on his lunch break. But as he stood pouring sparkling water for his lunch of fresh organic salad, he did so with the posture of one who can't go back. He was light-years away from where he'd come.

In her two-volume *Out of Order, Out of Sight*, Piper summarizes one aspect of Kant's work that so inspires her: "In order for us to make sense of experience at all, we have to categorize those experiences in terms of certain basic categories, which Kant thinks of as being innate. He says that categorizing experience in that way is a necessary condition for having a unified and internally integrated sense of self, so that if we did not categorize our experiences, we would be confronted with total chaos."

Initially, the basic requirements of being a gallery assistant suited me just fine. I loved making figure eights with a mop across the black wooden floors on winter days to clean away the salt tracked in by patrons' shoes. I loved drinking coffee in the ordered, peaceful silence where I was asked to photograph exhibits and write press releases. The art around me inspired me. It echoed what I can see, from a distance, as an essential quality of my boss. There was a sense of cleanliness, light, and loss in the small landscapes, abstract photographs, and glass sculptures that he chose to exhibit. It was like being surrounded by stylish ghosts—memories and relationships that have been blued or blotted, tarnished and refashioned over time. I also relished in the state-of-the-art sound system, which played good music at a volume as satisfying as the temperature of a perfect cup of tea. I loved the smell of the organic mushroom dressing my boss used every day on his salad. The neatness of the gallery prompted me to feel clearheaded and contained.

At the same time, though, something about the sharp lines made by hanging rulers, art books, desk edges, drawers of prints, stacks of paper, and matte cutters also separated me from some central aspect of the art world. I was privileged enough to wander around, but I felt left out. Or left behind to look surreptitiously through someone else's valuables, like a house sitter. I began to notice that this space was protected by an invisible fence of electric energy. It seemed that if I approached it at the wrong time, in the wrong manner, I might get into trouble.

The patrons who came in were easy to distinguish from the other locals. They were adults of any sex or ethnicity, but their clothes were tailored exactly to fit their forms. White, gray, and black outfits were accented by a very deliberate line, splash, or dot of color. Faces looked scrubbed and vibrant, and the manner in which our visitors walked had an air of ease and confidence. Conversations were more like lists or recitations—names of people, foreign countries, exhibitions, and institutions—that would hopefully elicit a warm crescendo of recognition from my boss. When he opened up to them, his back was toward me. He swung out his arms like two French doors.

On the night of an exhibit opening, I'd go to the bodega on the corner to purchase one particular kind of plastic cup that was especially clear and squat. I'd unwrap imported goat cheese from the local food co-op, take out the sharp knife from the bathroom, and lay these items out like a nurse would onto a wooden cutting board. I'd pour white wine that had been delivered that afternoon and make conversation.

Adrian Piper came from an African American family that had been divided into parts: there were those who were light enough to pass for white, and there were those too dark to try. Piper came from the latter bunch and never consciously attempted to infiltrate the highest echelons of society by encouraging the misconception that she was white. Her African American identity was one she'd learn to value, growing up. But she was light enough to be mistaken. She looked so white that she often overheard friends make offensive jokes about black people in the elevator. She would need, at one point or another, to inform new friends that she was black. There were distinct stages of dissonance and recovery in their reaction.

To hasten this process, she created calling cards to hand out to people. They stated, among other things: "Dear Friend, I am black."

Piper writes, "A benefit and a disadvantage of looking white is that most people treat you as though you were white. And so, because of how you've been treated, you come to expect this sort of treatment, not, perhaps, realizing that you're being treated this way because people think you're white, but falsely supposing, rather, that you're being treated this way because people think you are a valuable person."

Artists that contacted us for exposure usually fell into two distinct categories: they either had an MFA or they did not. The vast majority of people who fell into the latter category were rejected before they'd finished their pitch. There were more ways of identifying their fate than reading through a CV. If they looked like they could easily board a plane to Paris, they might have some hope. But if they stood in front of my desk long enough to need to put down their portfolio because their arms were tired, if they wore too much jewelry or had stains on their shirt, or were too old and seemed eager to talk to me even after realizing that I was just an assistant, they were probably not going to make the cut. I learned how to smile in a way that is probably common among pathological liars. If there was some other task I needed to get to, I wagged my hidden foot with impatience as they spoke. After a year of working there, I tended to put the portfolio they handed to me into a stack without looking at it as soon as the door shut behind them.

Piper's experience as an unseen black person was intrinsically linked to the graph-like nature of human mentality mentioned in Kant's *Critique of Pure Reason*. She felt that "most of the categories by which we make sense of our experience are poorly drawn rules of thumb" and "we get into trouble when the concrete particulars we distort or misidentify are other people."

Art that Piper created during this period worked to disrupt some of these false barriers separating people, and it even mocked the degree of distance Americans of different skin colors felt toward one another. In a series called "Vanilla Nightmares," Piper sketches black, monstrous figures onto the pages of the *New York Times*, figures who are in the process of attacking the white men and women in lingerie and credit-card advertisements and articles.

She also conducted "Funk Lessons," in which largely white audiences would learn, in the manner of a school lecture, how to dance to a genre of music generally associated with lower-class blacks.

At one point when I was working at the gallery, my mother called to tell me that my nephew had been put in prison for armed robbery.

The barrier between the so-called real world and the art world also bothered Piper. So she created art installations that overtly focused on how viewers would respond to her invitation of "real life news" into the gallery space.

In "Art for the Art World Surface Pattern," she wallpapers the interior of a small white room standing by itself in the center of a gallery with a collection of newspaper clippings and photographs from the *New York Times*. Featured stories, explains Piper, include "The Mexican Peon land takeover, the effects of the earthquake in Turkey, the student riots, beatings, and hangings in Thailand, riots and marches in South Africa, and so on." Text, stenciled in red, repeats on top of these images: "Not a Performance." A monologue is broadcast in the room, in which a voice impersonates potential responses that an art viewer might have to the work: "Christ, I really get enough of this stuff in the papers and on TV every day, you know? I really don't need this when I come to an art show. . . ."

Of such works, Piper says, "I want to identify well-known, knee-jerk unacceptable responses—not prescribe the politically correct one."

The woman who worked in the fabric store down the street came into the gallery to warn us that a group of African American teenagers had been robbing shopkeepers along the block, including her, at gunpoint. They were stealing computers. I thought about my nephew, and wondered what I would say if the group, as of yet uncaught, came into the gallery.

That night, I developed a speech in my head about the importance of a good education. I considered posting fliers around the neighborhood addressed to the three thieves, announcing that I hoped they used the computers they were taking to write their college applications. I felt as proficient with their reality as a good-natured white lady from the Wisconsin suburbs who'd become a fan of the *Fresh Prince of Bel Air*. The next day when a group of African American teenagers came in, I was alone in the gallery. My ears began to hum and my mind went blank.

In 1980, Piper created the installation "Four Intruders Plus Alarm System." A small, black room stands in the center of the exhibition floor. There are four light boxes hanging, each with a silkscreened photograph of a black man staring directly at the viewer. Light does not shine through these images uniformly; it is concentrated around the men's eyes, causing their expressions to seem especially intense.

Underneath the boxes there is a set of headphones, each with a different monologue playing. In one, a voice says, "It seems as though this piece is meant to shock me out of my composure, and it just doesn't succeed in doing that, because what I'm looking for when I come into a gallery is an art experience." In another, "I'm simply antagonized by the hostility of this piece. . . . She's representing all blacks as completely hostile and alienated, and I just think that that's not true." And, "Oh this is . . . this is really right on . . . I know what it's like to really feel angry at everybody on the street because they're just not digging where you're at, you know." And "It's not my responsibility. It's not my fault that things are bad for some members of this society . . . everyone's responsible for their own environment and their own lives, and my feeling is that, you know, they leave me alone and I'll leave them alone."

Piper was surprised to find that many visitors did not detect the satirical nature of the piece. "While the black audience, and some members of the white audience, understood the devices immediately, others thanked me for expressing their views so eloquently."

My desk was all the way across the gallery, in the back, several yards from the door. I greeted the boys when they came in, wanting to believe that they just so happened to be the first, black fourteen-year-olds to visit for art's sake. But realistically speaking, the gallery never enticed the kinds of people who had lived in the neighborhood before the middle-class whites arrived. The expression in their eyes was shocking to me— these young men were still very much, boys. I watched them with unbridled curiosity for a while, though my body was churning with adrenaline.

The art didn't seem to interest them much. When they made it over to my desk they did not give it the same respectful distance that other patrons would. One of the boys draped his arms across the shoulder-level ledge and gazed down. They seemed nervous, like me, and began to ask little questions. But as we spoke, I could see that we were all zoomed out of the experience, that our voices were muted, and this was just the first act in a charade. Part of me felt like a misguided idiot for sitting on the other side of the desk, like a greedy child with her arms wrapped around her belongings. What was I doing protecting this space from them? At what point in history or geography had it become OK for us to be so separate from one another? I was ashamed that my life had come to this. I considered reaching down, unplugging the cord, handing over the computer and giving them a wink.

"OK guys," I said, standing quickly. "I hate to make you go, but I have to run down the street for an errand. I need to lock the gallery."

One boy was thin and had acne. Another wore a red shirt. For a moment they hadn't seemed sure that they were going to listen to me. They turned around slowly and began to drift like floating sheets of paper toward the door. The slowest of the three held out his index finger and traced it along the stretch of white wall as he passed, leaving an invisible streak of himself underneath the hanging photographs.

Later that day, my boss congratulated me for thinking so quickly on my feet. But the gallery felt different after that. The lines that once traversed the space with precision began to seem severe. Times were tough and we could no longer afford a cleaning lady, which meant that dust began to collect on the empty, even planes of white space.

Adrian Piper says, "Someone who tries to maintain personal authenticity by adhering to *any* circumscribed social or ethnic role will tend to view liberation from that role—anyone's liberation—as a personal threat." During one of her exhibitions, a white male viewer began a fight with her dealer. He threw chairs around and started shouting: he was white and he was going to stay that way.

Piper says, "I am cornered, hemmed in, somewhere in the basement of the building, prepared to crash my way out. My art practice is a reflecting mirror of light and darkness, a high sunny window that holds out to me the promise of release into night." It has been rumored that students and colleagues at Wellesley College felt that Adrian Piper became more and more socially awkward in her tenure there as a professor. The homepage of her current Web site shows what looks like a photograph taken at the moment she propelled herself, finally, from the disturbed social reality she spent so much of her life trying to disrupt: a small girl waves from a miniature space craft as it moves in the direction of a star-cluttered universe.

Before moving to New York, my girlfriend and I spent the summer in Alaska. We carried plastic jugs of water up a hill to a two-story wood cabin with no running water or electricity. Quiet evenings were spent eating vegetables from handmade ceramic bowls and drinking growlers full of beer from the local brewery. We entertained ourselves by watching a pregnant moose graze outside the massive windows, and because there were only ever a few hours of darkness in a day, we never managed to see the sun set fully. I practiced yoga in a studio that overlooked the Kachemak Bay and worked at a bookstore co-owned by a brother and sister. I biked fast down the hill from our cabin. When I approached the edge of the road as I circled down, the glacier sticking out from the bay seemed only inches from my skin, a naked jewel that adorned my quiet life.

But I am unsettled by the fact that I have been at liberty to breathe such rarefied air while my nephew waits out what has become, for black young men in this country, the inevitability of a prison term. He has been convicted, again, and is only at the beginning of a sentence longer than what the Capeman, Salvador Agron, ultimately served for murder. I have begun to tell him about meditation as a way to combat the flat, long landscape of time that surrounds him. In one of the songs from their musical, "Time Is an Ocean," Paul Simon and Derek Walcott depict the atmosphere of prison in a kind of warped pastoral, the racialized mockery of a bucolic setting: "A forest and a prison/ where the snow and guards are white." Their musical manages to be a silly cliché, but the politics of race and class it meant to protest have not changed. It is impossible for me to imagine my nephew transposed onto an Alaskan landscape without first imagining the chart we call reality, the system of boxes we live inside, the bright, white-blue glacier of nature as we know it, collapsing.

Grahamstown, South Africa

Cicatrization

The *New York Times* has warned me that the image I'm about to see is graphic. But I press the tiny arrow long before processing this, in a compulsive expression of my animal self. And so it is that I am staring at Gaddafi's body, a little underwhelmed, a little surprised by the flicker of pleasure I feel at the specter of his disorientation, his bloodied wounds. I don't think of myself as reacting this way to violence. Normally I avoid these kinds of images, and I certainly don't seek them out. I am disturbed by the fact that anyone's death could be framed, as Gaddafi's is, as Bin Laden's was, by such cartoonish glee.

This image from Libya is a kind of synecdoche, part for the whole of Africa. My associations with this continent are all present on Gaddafi's face: a momentous, historical bleeding. The wound and the rupture. At the thought of Africa, I am once again suspended in the shock of violence, the terror and the beauty of life jostling its way out of bewildered flesh like a bird busting its way out of a cardboard box. Red lines sliced, skin wrapped tight around the exact shape of a bone, gashes blown into the surface of the body. What is the difference between these things and Africa?

As a child I sprawled out on the living room floor, paging through coffee table books wherein the gourds, instruments, necklaces, and masks we had hanging on our walls and bookshelves were carried, played, and worn by actual people. Flipping through *Africa Adorned*, I traced my finger over the bodies covered with white ash or intricate scarification. I tried on the beaded necklaces that my father had collected over time, looking at photographs of women with tight metal coils around their arms and necks. In the Mangbetu tribe, skulls were, until the 1950s, "elongated as a process of beautification." The photograph of an infant shows the result of a procedure whereby, "soon after birth a baby's head was either confined between two pieces of wood or bound tightly with strips of bark."

Angela Fisher writes, "Boys and girls of the Murle, a small group of people living in Southern Sudan, have their faces and part of their chests scarred with intricate circular patterns in a process known as cicatrization. In this, a sort of bas-relief tattoo, the skin is pierced and the wound rubbed with ash so that it becomes inflamed and later heals as a hard scar in relief." In one black-and-white photograph, the torso of a Sara woman from Chad is knit like a blanket, raised marks in parallel lines or twisting in loops at the hips of a diamond that stems from her protruding belly button, which is not a circle but an almost rectangular bulge that wears thick hatch mark whiskers, three to each side. This is a kind of violence that has nothing to do with aggression. Rather, it is evidence of connection with the spiritual world.

Some of the tribes depicted, like the Dogon tribe of Mali, filed their teeth in reference to the celestial twins of their origin story, the "Nommo," who were responsible for creating their race. Dogon men and women would shape their teeth in order to "recall the origin of speech, believed to have started as the weaving of threads through the sharply filed teeth of the Nommo, and women wore nose studs and lip rings which symbolized the bobbin and shuttle used in that mythical weaving." Wind of words pushing past the raw nerve of exposed bone as a way to honor the very act of expression.

Other tribes used lip plates or plugs, stretching for example the mouths of Sara women so that, as the story goes, slave traders would be too frightened to steal their bodies. Seeing, perhaps, the devil inside of them reflected in that gaping mouth.

When I tell people I am going to South Africa, the unanimous response involves an intake of breath. I am lectured about the startling statistics for rape there. Cautioned to be careful in one hundred different ways, many nonverbal. But my hunger for this experience is heightened by the dullness I've been feeling of late. I am spiritually numb, moving from art classes to the subway to work to home with little curiosity or excitement. I wonder if the notion of violence, at least of extremity, is part of what drives me toward Africa, some inclination to be jolted back to the realm of sensation.

A few months before I decide to apply for the study abroad program, I wander through the Whitney Museum's retrospective, entitled "Ana Mendieta: Earth Body," witnessing the artist's work for the first time. In a review of this exhibition, Mark Stevens writes, "Mendieta summons the ancients without flinching: She wants to feel the spray of blood on her skin."

Ana Mendieta was sent by her parents from Cuba to the United States in 1961 through Operation Peter Pan. Before her mother could join them, she and her sister spent years moving from foster home to foster home. Eventually, she enrolled as an art student at the University of Iowa.

Critics like Coco Fusco say that when Mendieta burned, dug, or painted the earth with blood and tempera in the shape of her body, it was in attempt to reconnect with nature. The artist herself acknowledged her work as an appropriation from Yoruba culture, of Santeria's "healing imagery," an act that might connect her to the past, as she sought "to overcome limits of time, space and mortality."

But as I look at her work, the invocation of violence through burning and blood, I find a familiar mode of connecting to some far-gone homeland. Not just because it reminds me of afternoons spent flipping through pages of those rites of passage but because of all the other ways that Africa has bled. Through the simulation of bodies breaking, her artwork calls to mind the fracturing that history has imposed upon flesh—the pain that either moved our ancestors to this country in the first place, or that which ruptured their bodies in transit. For my own conception of ancestry, this means the movement through time of black bodies over ocean and to the fields, a dotted line stretching across the map from some unknown country in Africa all the way to Alabama. The very thought of such a passage is one so twisted as to turn prose into gibberish in Toni Morrison's *Beloved*, to set Thandie Newton's naked form to shakes and screaming.

I covered my eyes when my parents took me to see Whoopi Goldberg star in the musical about South Africa, *Sarafina*, but can still feel the vibrations of violence in the ghost image of the darkened seats in front of us. I can still see the African elephants whose tusks have been ripped out of their faces in the video for Michael Jackson's "Earth Song." Then there is the swing and curve of weapons in story after story of cleft appendages in Sierra Leone and spilled organs on the soil beneath Rwanda's civil war. After a while, I stopped listening, learned to hear these screams as all others, too far away and enormous to register as much more than white noise.

In *Africa Adorned*, Angela Fisher writes that government officials were wary of having the "primitive" traditions of the tribal cultures photographed, and went to great lengths to hide them from the lens. She remembers, "So sensitive is this issue that on one occasion when I was recording an important ceremony attended by 10,000 nomads in a remote corner of the West African savannah, a certain Minister of the Interior ordered my arrest, and in the middle of the night I was taken without warning by a police escort and forced to leave the country."

Every time she came back, there was less visual evidence of the traditions she had seen only months before. "On successive visits to the isolated Dinka people in the Nile swamps of Sudan, I noticed that in a matter of months these proud nomads, traditionally naked except for a covering of ash and body beads, had, like many others on the continent, begun to wear synthetic head scarves, motif T-shirts, and even platform-heel shoes obtained from visiting traders." My parents' coffee table books document the moment of shift from what Africa used to be to what it has become.

It is a documentary made in the early nineties that made me want to visit Africa, years before I actually went. I had the scene in my mind of a dance or a party where young people wore brand names on green and purple T-shirts, composing outfits with the same finesse as the women of *African Canvas*, who painted patterns on the walls of a public shrine only a few years before. In the film, the logo, color, and sheen of soda cans were recycled into the fabric of the objects and the background, making a Rauschenberg-like composition so vibrant and rooted in a historical process so particular that I had to see it face-to-face. What I didn't realize was that this collaged life was the aftermath of a resounding, widespread cultural death. Margaret Courtney-Clarke, the photojournalist who created *African Canvas*, writes, "The art I found was so extraordinary that it could not go unnoticed. It was also disappearing rapidly, as if a door—synchronized to my shutter speed—was closing after each exposure."

In *Regarding the Pain of Others*, Susan Sontag describes a series of photographs taken in Cambodia by record keepers for the Khmer

Rouge. Every person who was to be executed had to sit for a photograph just before dying. Sontag compares these men, women, and children to "the Flaying of Marsyas," where "Apollo's knife is eternally about to descend." The subjects of these photographic portraits are "forever looking at death, forever about to be murdered, forever wronged."

When we flew from JFK, I didn't read Mandela's *Long Walk to Freedom* like my classmates. I watched a Will Smith film and a South African movie about Miriam Makeba. And I slept so much that the lithe, Senegalese stewards began to make fun of me. "She's awake!" one shouted to the other when I opened my eyes before our descent. But their teasing was gentle, and the sight of Dakar from the window sweet as I gazed through the fogged lens of near sleep. A group of middle-aged musicians boarded the plane in Senegal, wearing robes of bright colors and laughing heartily. I landed on the continent the way that so many black Americans before me have. Like the speaker in Countee Cullen's poem "Heritage," my entire body swam in the sense of wholeness that only an abstract notion can offer, the purity of the mythical return: "What is Africa to me;/ Copper sun or scarlet sea,/ Jungle star or jungle track,/ Strong bronzed men, or regal black." But as the plane rose again, inching closer to South Africa, I felt an insidious kind of knowing. That Africa means one thing in the mind and something very different when you walk upon it. This is the place where, for example, Langston Hughes was informed that he was white.

"I don't want to leave here," the young, African girl beside me had whispered to her mother as the plane lifted off in New York.

Standing inside the airport in Cape Town, I looked through the opening and closing doors near baggage claim with mounting terror, as though we were on a space station and the black night outside was pure, dark infinity. I noticed myself thinking: *so long as there are still white people around, we are safe.* At which point I knew that I was facing things within myself I hadn't had to see before. Africa was going to be my reckoning. With what I still can't name.

Mendieta's work is fraught with absent figures. The shape of a body dug out of the earth or indented in a riverbed, set on fire, splashed with red paint or filled with smoldering ash. When she was thirty-six, she fell to her death from a New York City apartment, calling to mind the imprint her own body would have made had it encountered the earth instead of the roof of the deli where she landed. Each piece that she composed—her naked body covered with flowers, a giant woman's figure set aflame one night in Mexico—inadvertently commemorates her own passing, these ceremonies and faux burials a kind of preparation. As if to say: *I knew it was coming.*

The debate over the cause of her death often invokes the name of her husband, the artist Carl Andre, who some fear may have forced her out the window. Much of Mendieta's work gives this hypothesis a kind of grisly foundation: *Untitled (Self-Portrait with Blood)* is a series of six shots of the artist with blood coming from her hairline and nose, as though it had been taken by a doctor or policeman following a domestic abuse call.

In 1973, when she was still in school, Mendieta was found crouched over a table, her lower body stripped of clothes and bloody, her belongings disordered in the apartment around her. It was a performance piece she would later call "Untitled (Rape Scene)," a response to the violent rape and murder of a University of Iowa student on her campus.

In *Blood Tracks*, she dips her hands in blood and drags them down the wall, making a Y shape on the white surface as her body moves slowly toward the floor.

As easy as it is to project some morbid telepathy onto the artist, or even to wonder if she dabbled too much with the other side, tipping her chances, letting herself be moved toward it, this was not what was happening. At least, I don't believe that the world works this way. Facing death is not the same thing as inviting it.

When we went for a tour of the Langa township in Capetown, my group of mostly graduate student peers and I debated the ethics of raising our cameras. The environment was ripe for documentation—rich in *National Geographic* golds, rusted aluminum, hand-painted signs, miscegenated green eyes that provided sweet contrast with caramel skin and a backdrop of aimless, rusty wires and peeling blue paint. It was too dark inside for me to take a decent shot of the sleek metal of a kettle on the stove in the kitchen of a house that was a room, one that fifteen people shared. (It is worth repeating that this is a thought I had: *Damn. It's too dark.* About film.) Babies walked through indiscernible pools of a liquid with gorgeous, forebodingly vibrant copper hues.

Sontag refers frequently to Goya's sequence of etchings entitled "The Disasters of War," depicting Napoleon's invasion of Spain in 1808. It is not Goya's images only that capture Sontag's curiosity but their short captions, which read: *One cannot look; This is bad; This is worse; This is the worst! Barbarians! What madness! This is too much! Why? I saw this; This is the truth.*

I went with my mother on a church-facilitated trip to an orphanage in Tijuana when I was a child. I remember the location more than the people: the walls outside the orphanage, the beach we went to with the children, the way the ocean and the air were the color of desert camouflage as we all just seemed to stand there. The day, or at least my memory of it, hits the same emotional chord as Christian Bale's lip-synching scene in *Empire of the Sun*, the one where he sings the Welsh lullaby "Suo Gan" through the barbed wire of an internment camp to a group of Japanese kamikaze pilots. I know I'm not the only child of the eighties who has only to hear the first four notes of this song before beginning to cry.

As we wandered through Langa, I felt the opposite sensation—no echo chamber of empathy. I was newly numb. The whole enterprise felt fake. We were travelers, led by a guide, in the throes of a debate about "poverty tourism." Sure, we were ashamed by the speed with which we jockeyed for certain shots, or walked away from others, as though the compositions we framed and the angle from which we captured that same woman's face, or the joy we were able to solicit from that child's throat made any one of us less corrupt than the other. There was no danger, not to us, no promise that documentation could lead to any sort of relief for those portrayed. It felt like we were cheating at something. Certainly cheating the children by convincing ourselves that because they said they wanted to be photographed they should. But also cheating ourselves as we stepped gingerly around the people whose homes we toured.

Let me be clear: we were not unkind. We spoke with people, we asked questions, we held hands with children. The professor who led us had been an ardent activist under apartheid, during which time she risked her life every day until she was forced to leave the country. I had respect for the members of our group, many of whom taught in New York City public schools. But we were caught up in something that felt more than a little bit awful. Audubon's beautiful depiction of a bird becomes gruesome when we are told that those birds were killed in order for him to sketch them; pinned back into life-like poses. I shot one photograph of two girls playing, and seeing it now, I am struck by the movement captured there—at once playful, violent, and inert. It reminds me of the hug two men might make as they fall injured upon one another, standing in embrace before slouching slowly to the ground.

In the excursions that followed, my lens started to turn downward and off to the side. To Mandela's toilet. To the hand of a former prisoner from Robben Island as it held a wooden pole. To the shadow that letters on a glass door made as they slanted onto the floor.

"I was confused," I wrote in my journal, "by the amount of scars I saw on the faces of the children on the boat today. One boy had a scar as thick as a caterpillar on his head." These scars had nothing to do with cicatrization. It was my way of saying, in response to all this injury: *how is it that I have been spared?*

A YouTube video shows a man holding an ax. He grabs a white chicken and quickly, expertly applies its weight to the bird's neck. He hands it to a naked Ana Mendieta, whose hair is parted down the middle in a ponytail. She stands in front of a white wall in what looks to be a basement studio somewhere in Iowa. She holds the chicken away from her body, clearly struggling with the frenetic redistribution of its weight in space. It is upside down as its blood spills onto her, onto itself, and onto the floor, convulsing, flapping. I am surprised by the strength the bird's decapitated body shows, feel as though I'm watching the shoulder blades and wingspan of a much larger beast as it opens and closes its body with no apparent slowing.

My friend Arianne recently met a new lover. On her way home from that first encounter with him, she passed a car that had rammed into a cow. "It was gruesome," she tells me. She got out to see if everything was all right, and went with the two young men to verify that the animal was, in fact, dead. They called the police together before she began driving again, into a night that was as dark as the cow's black body.

Two weeks later, on her way back to visit this new love, she took a train. The train slowed, all of a sudden, because it had hit a cow. "We could hear cracking and splintering underneath the wheels," she told me, "and I said to myself: well, that's what bones sound like."

A few days after she returned, I could hear her digging a hole in the backyard across the street. Something about the action seemed menacing. Like a coward, I hurried inside, because I knew she wasn't starting a garden. I asked her about it later. "Oh that," she said, caught up in a thrust of tears as though lambasted by the wind. "I was burying a cat." She had woken up to the sound of her dogs tearing it apart. "What is going *on?*" She asked, referring to the cat and the cows. Both of us tensed up with the thought that these deaths had to mean something horrible.

During this same period of time, I was trying to stop smoking so much weed. I did Tai Chi for the first time, at which point I felt overwhelmed by a warmth that was indescribably strong. Grateful, I decided to go on a juice fast, to mark a transition into what I hoped would be a healthier lifestyle. That same day, I walked outside to startle a small owl, who looked up at me from the middle of the street in front of my house. It was standing on top of a pile of feathers, which was not a pile of feathers but the bloodied body of the pigeon it had just killed. Predator clutched prey and flew off to a nearby curb to finish the job. In front of Arianne's house.

As I biked away, I told myself, *that had to have been a hawk. It's still daylight.* But as I replayed the scene in my head, I saw the startled expression again and I swear it was worn by a pair of owl eyes. I told all this to a friend, who studies Chinese medicine. After looking up the owl in her book of animal totems, she told me: "If you have seen an owl you are being asked to use your powers of keen, silent observation to intuit some life situation. Owl is befriending you and aiding you in seeing the whole truth. Owl can bring you messages in the night through dreams or meditation. Pay attention to the signals and omens. The truth always brings further enlightenment." Every time I passed the carcass of that pigeon, rather than feeling foreboding or fear, I felt a weird sense of affirmation. A cosmic pat on the back.

In the Afro-Cuban tradition of Santeria, chickens, pigeons, doves, ducks, guinea pigs, turtles, goats, or sheep are often sacrificed as an offering to the god Orisha. A sacrifice might be performed to honor birth, death, or marriage or to initiate some sort of healing.

In the Ana Mendieta video, entitled "Chicken Piece," the bird's body quiets for brief periods before trying again to fly, so that the artist must tighten every muscle in her body to keep it steady, caught in space, headless. One critic asked whether or not this piece was very successful, as if two women standing by the banks of a river could be deemed unsuccessful in their own, undocumented sacrifice to Orisha. But even if it was an artist in a basement and not a healer standing on a Cuban shore, it still happened: there was this gift.

A soothsayer in an animist society of tribal Africa might, according to Angela Fisher, counsel a man who has killed a cow: "Go and have a ring made with the motif of a cow to replace the animal you have slain." So many ancient traditions view death not as a threat but as a ritualistic tool, a knife's slice through the skin of space and time, the wound of which might cast our lives in deeper relief, offering the occasion to say (of new love, of clarity): *I saw this. This is the truth.*

A Zen teacher once told me that guilt is not a useful feeling. It is an emotion wholly at the service of the ego. Melancholy or frustration are emotions that more usefully move us through the process of inhabiting, understanding, or potentially preventing another person's pain. But when we feel guilty, we are drawing attention to ourselves, even if it is for the purposes of punishment. *I caused this. I let this happen. How could I have been so stupid.* Meanwhile, there is still the limp body, or the crying child, the hurt lover, the abandoned friend.

It seems to me a particularly American impulse to see another person's suffering as an indictment. This is one reason that racism is so hard for many Americans to handle. So famously litigious, we are caught up in the blame game and don't always know how to rise above it. *Slavery. . . . Isn't that conversation over yet? Haven't we given that its fair due? What do you want from me? Can't we get over it?* But most of us have yet to say we're sorry, because we don't want to admit we did anything wrong. And most of the time, no one said we did. Africa falls into a similar trap, tripping off our defensiveness. We are tired of feeling responsible for something we didn't really do in the first place. *Africa again? Is it even allowed to make the front pages anymore?* The enormity of that suffering is so large that, because we can't personally fix it, we cease to want to face it.

At one point, at the University of Cape Town, our group was "invited to a conference about study abroad excursions." I use quotation marks because it felt more like being lured into a lion's den on the pretense that there would be free food. These were the Bush years, so Americans abroad were given a lot of crap, regardless of their voting record. We sat through a panel of lectures by South African professors who complained about American elitism and privilege for hours. We waited in the audience, furious, anxious for the chance to defend ourselves. They'd rant, chuckle, roll their eyes, crease their brows, assemble their papers, and then the next speaker would get up to do the exact same thing. I still get annoyed when I think of this day. We didn't vote for Bush! We aren't the frat kids who come to South Africa and refuse to leave their dorms! We don't demand better living conditions than actual South African students! Feet were a-shakin' and hearts beat so loud with pre-hand-raising jitters that the room thumped.

At lunch, I spoke to a black South African administrator from a historically black, rural college who complained that his students didn't even wear shoes. It was funny for him to hear his compatriots whine about the Americans who may have been annoying, sure, but at least they brought in money. I rubbed my hands together and scribbled in my notebook. When we assembled again for more, post-lunch ranting, I raised my hand to speak. I suggested that, instead of worrying about Americans, wealthier South African universities should do study abroad exchanges with historically black and poor South African universities. My voice was shaking. To this day, I am proud of my point, even if it was a deflection. But I also made the mistake of calling the kind administrator with whom I'd shared my lunch by the wrong name. In fact, I called him by the name of the president of Zimbabwe, Mr. Mugabe, so that the poignancy of my comment was lost, along with my credibility, in the hilarity of my error. When I remember this, my brain moves easily back into that defensive loop, laughing to itself while it mutters: "Ha! funny to hear all this from a bunch of white South African men. Did we ask them how they spent their time under apartheid? Did we turn around and blame them for their country?" I too was raised to play the blame game.

In her essay "All Apologies," Eula Biss brings up the instances in which nations have and have not been able to apologize for acts of extreme violence or persecution. She also describes instances during her childhood in which she did something wrong and had to confront the prospect of apologizing. I love the childhood self she admits to here, one that is scheming, resentful, and unabashedly bad. She shows us the moments when historical leaders have used crafty syntax to avoid owning up, incapable for legal reasons of just saying the words: we're sorry. She also tells a more recent, personal story from her time teaching in New York City. "A boy hissed at me in the hall while I was on my way to the bathroom. As I spun around, angry, I realized that he might have thought I was another student." Later on, in the principal's office, she waited reluctantly for her boss to retrieve the child who had offended her. When he arrived, it was the wrong boy. She told him so. "'Yeah,' he said as he pulled down his baseball cap and started to walk away, 'but it might have been my cousin.'"

At the end of the essay, she writes, "I apologize for slavery." And it's hard to imagine that such a sentence could mean anything anymore, when no one among us is personally responsible, and none of those who suffered are still alive. She finishes by saying, "It wasn't me, true. But it might have been my cousin." And something about this gesture floors me, still moves me to tears. It makes me think of every skeptical expression that has ever reacted silently to a comment I have made about racism. "But," this expression says, fraught with the friction of one wrongly accused. "But," the narrowed or rolled eyes and held breath say, before letting out a sigh that means "Never mind."

I wonder if we have started to assume that because we *do* become desensitized we *must* become desensitized. We are socialized to think of emotionality in the face of death (removed death, distant death) as naive. But there is some relief, perhaps, in retaining a child's sense of innocence in the face of this thing we hide from daily but think we are inured to. Aren't we still allowed to feel sad or strange about it, even if it's always? Even if it's Gaddafi?

There is a man named Johnny who drives a cab. The first time that he drove us between Johannesburg and Pretoria, he gave us his card, and so I spend several hour-long car rides beside him, listening to his thoughts about Xhosa warriors, educating his son, fighting for his country in the Orange Free State. So many of the college students I spoke with in Pretoria were tired of talking about apartheid. They didn't want to hear another question about race ever again. Their history had been reduced to the size of an infomercial, a tourist's guide book, the bumper sticker for which they were known to the world. But to Johnny, the wounds would always be fresh. As would the victories. He lives in a constant state of gratitude for what came to pass. "There are pictures of Mandela that we have never *seen*," he says one afternoon, pounding a palm on the dash, his heart pressed up in emphasis against the steering wheel.

One day, a man sat at the head of a table in a conference room. He admitted that he'd never done this kind of thing before. It was our own, small Truth and Reconciliation commission. He knew our professor, who had also lived through apartheid, though she fought against it and was black. He, on the other hand, was white, a member of the security police. To see the two of them laugh in private congress with each other was astonishing, and for a moment, commission enough.

He had electrocuted a man's genitals. He hadn't felt as though he'd had a choice. *You grow up in this certain way, believing certain things.* This was not a polished speech by any means. I don't know whether or not he practiced what he was going to say to us beforehand. His wife and children did not know that he was there.

I thought we were all astonished by the fact that he'd made it there in the first place, and so watched in silent awe. But other things were being felt in the room. The girl beside him began to cry at one point and did not ever stop. She didn't do much about it, either, letting snot and tears fall onto her chest. When he got the chance, our speaker turned and touched her arm, asked if she was all right. At which point a ferocious sense of love sprang up in me, though it was a bit aimless. Meanwhile, my classmates were practicing for their roles in an Al Pacino movie: *If you did that to my family man I'd kill you before you saw what was coming.* Bile and pomp and anger and recrimination. At first I felt sorry for him and annoyed with them: didn't they *get it*? Forgiveness is bigger than vengeance. I took my lessons from *Free to Be You and Me* so seriously. But at one point or another, I started to see: this was why he had come. The whole episode, especially their anger, was a tonic — worth whole years of therapy he'd otherwise never seek.

I wrote down my own question: why was rape used as a tactic of intimidation if one of the primary concerns of the apartheid government was racial purity? I wanted to know how the rapists themselves came to terms with this. For some reason, I did not assume that it was a matter of *if* he had raped black women, so much as *when*. When I asked him, he responded, "I wish I could tell you," which is a way of saying, "that is something I did not do." I don't know why this surprised me so much. I guess because the story in my head had become so true to me. He was, now, my crying classmate's absent white father, and she his child of rape, his abandoned biracial baby, and even though they were only symbols for these things, that portrait meant more to me than almost any other thing I saw in South Africa. I saw it as evidence that the world has a way of offering up its own host of totems or ghosts in case we ever feel like it's time to face them.

It doesn't take long for the muggings to start. One person from our group is robbed at an ATM in Cape Town. The other is in Pretoria, walking down the street, when he is forced into a car and taken to an ATM. The group of men ask him to remove all of his cash. He remembers that Africans have utmost respect for their elders, so tells them that his grandmother is sick. He had been on his way to buy medicine for her. Could he keep a bit of cash for her prescription? Of course, they tell him, yes.

The point of our program is to study education and social reform, so we spend a good amount of time at various schools. I interview one white male teacher. He says his house is robbed constantly. He is afraid to walk places. He is afraid for his family. He wants to move to Australia. I am always surprised at how quickly white South Africans confide their fear and distrust of black Africans to us, even when we wear black skin.

I go jogging in the mornings, past the well-to-do homes near our guest house, the walls of which are topped with broken glass and twisted bits of metal. But I don't feel calmed by the exercise, as I never let go into the movement. I am always ready to turn back, convinced I've gone too far, caught like a rabbit on the red dust between irrationally drawn, invisible zones of safety and danger. One afternoon,

I walk by myself from the wealthy neighborhood where we live to Pretoria's city center. I have no idea how long this walk is—half an hour? An hour? Two? Because it lasts for my entire life. The wealthy homes become more humble. The cars and traffic increase. What surrounds me is familiar, and if I let my mind wander, I could be walking toward downtown Minneapolis or downtown Los Angeles, except, I keep telling myself: this is Africa. This is Africa. This is Africa. I blur my eyes, some Dorothy who doesn't realize what she's wishing for, clicking my heels, subconsciously willing upon myself the thing that I fear most: for Africa to become itself. To stop pretending already. Which means some kind of violence.

There is a series of four shots in which Ana Mendieta is shown wearing a white long-sleeved shirt and gray pants. She is standing outside, on a city street, her hair down, in front of a white wall. Gathering red paint from a pan on the ground, she uses her hand to smear an outline loosely around the contours of her body on the wall. Inside of the shape, she uses her hand to write the words *There is a devil inside me*.

Multiple witnesses have posted videos online of college students who sit peacefully, arms linked, as a man in a black suit wearing a riot helmet shows the crowd a red can. The Occupy Wall Street movement has taken over UC Davis. The police officer shakes the can, as though this is a magic show and the kids assembled are only there to be entertained. But then he presses down. Orange pepper spray descends upon young bodies who sit less than a foot away from him. Some of their faces are tilted downward, some stay lifted. People are screaming for the man to stop. I wait for another body dressed in black to interfere, but these actions are all part of a plan. Experts who speak on behalf of the police force assure us that, indeed, this kind of behavior is completely normal. Apparently the officers felt trapped.

What is so shocking is the way that the policemen react to their own actions. They exactly resemble a malignant tumor, clustering with a ridiculous, unifying fear into a wobbling mass, pushed by the protesting students toward the edge of the quad. Each officer faces outward, with a face full of terror, arms holding up riot gear and batons. "Shame on you," the students chant. The officers brace themselves. In a normal world, when you act out as they have done, when you do something wrong to somebody else—to somebody else's child—you cover your head and wait for the blow. What is so terrible to see, like the body of that withering witch, is the process by which their own fear deforms them. The students cheer when the officers leave, but I don't imagine a similar response in the hearts of the departed.

After apartheid ended, after the violence inflicted upon the majority population of black, Malay, and Coloured bodies, many whites could not believe that the country they had wronged would not descend upon them.

One day, three of us take an excursion. The woman who sat next to me on the plane offers to drive us from Port Elizabeth into the country, toward the festival in Grahamstown. "There have been muggings," she tells me, speaking of knives and guns. She gives me her phone number, worried that we haven't yet found a place to stay. By nightfall my panic has grown like a hysterical pregnancy. I can hardly see straight during the play we see that night, my breath has become so irregular. I don't remember being introduced to the cast, can hardly recall the trip we made to some campus where there might still be floor space left for us to sleep on. Nobody seems to mind that it is dark out, that somebody might want to hurt us. All I want is a door to lock. Eventually, we find a room in an overpriced hotel. My friends leave to go on a ghost tour of the city, returning late that night with stories of dancing and flirtation. I smile like a wax figurine, as they tell their stories, sick with fear in a bed that doesn't make me feel any safer, angry at my mind for what it has done to me.

During the day, we wander the festival by ourselves. Two policewomen patrol the stalls of a bathroom as I wash my hands. Whole periods of time are fine: I see art, I see plays, I laugh or cry with aesthetic appreciation. There are world-class performances and photography exhibitions and it is clearly magical. I sit on a hill at one point, enjoying the expanse of what surrounds me. I turn my head to see the window of a white house. The sliver of interior, colorful art on the walls cast with afternoon light beckons me to come live there, as in that moment everything exactly resembles the story of an Africa I learned from Ladysmith Black Mambazo. I eat, I write, I go for walks, but panic overtakes me like bouts of nausea, waves of it rattling through my head, turning my face into a mask of pure suspicion. I see myself reflected in the way people look at me. A twenty-something black man laughing with his friends begins to grimace as I pass by. He is standing only a couple of feet away when he raises a water gun and shoots me point-blank in the face.

There are many scenes of departure in South Africa. In one, for example, our group boards a van to leave Venda. "Don't give them candy," someone has warned us. And I don't think I did. But something happens that made the children crowd around me. Maybe I let them play with my camera. Whatever it is, they want more. One child asks me for my name. As the engine revs and we begin to drive away, dozens of children surround the vehicle and together, they begin to call after me. I do not know what to do with my face, to hide it or smile, to make eye contact with anyone, or just look out the window and wave. The sound of their voices feels overwhelming, but it is not an exclusively joyous occasion. A few minutes into our journey, someone begins to pass around a bottle of antiseptic gel. One of our classmates fumes for a while before reprimanding us. "I didn't see anybody asking for Purell after we spent all afternoon petting a pack of filthy lions," she says, and it feels so good in the haze of ambiguous emotions to be told, for once, what to feel, even if that is shame. As the children's voices echo in my head, my own name feels like a kind of taunt.

I first see them on the street in front of our fancy hotel in Grahamstown, frozen in mechanical poses. Boys who wear ash on their faces, or paint. Sometimes you walk by and the street is a garden of painted human statues, eyes fixated on no point in space, arms in holey sweaters, bare elbows jutting mechanically, chests bent forward, stomachs fluttering for breath. There is a box on the ground, and if you put change inside of it, the boys begin to dance. Their face paint mimics the culture that so many of us have come to Africa expecting, but their dance revives our own, American history, mimicking minstrel shows and soft shoe shuffling. "I just want to give you money," I say, trying to give them change without soliciting this ugly performance, which feels like the violent storm of all our histories bombarding against each other on the pavement. But they dance. Even when I beg them not to.

At one point, I take a photograph of a group of the small boys near the edge of the market, gathering with toy machine guns over a green metal trash can with a fire inside of it. They are so small, their clothes torn and dirty, their eyes so divorced from the adult world around them. "Are you hungry?" I ask a couple of kids, feeling a rumble in my own stomach. They nod in unison. So I buy them a sausage sandwich and cut it into three pieces to share. Another boy appears, a bit older, and I get him something too. It seems as though I have risen above my panic at this point, and I visit stalls in the market on a high of relief and gratitude. It will soon be time to go.

When I meet up with my friend, two boys who can't be more than seven or eight years old walk at some distance behind us. "This is wrong," Claire says as I hasten my pace, looking behind at them obsessively. "I know," I say. But there aren't many people around. Tents have been disassembled. The two boys behind us are the only people in sight. Panic drives me forward. In a moment that will haunt me for years afterward, I begin to walk faster still. To my friend's disgust, I actually start to run.

In the graphic novel *Who Is Ana Mendieta*, a newspaper article describes the account of a doorman who heard shouting right before the artist fell to her death. He heard the words "No, no, no," and "don't." But, he testified, this man felt that the voice that pleaded was not helpless. There was, in it, "some kind of self confidence." Her form, that inextinguishable self, her many *siluetas*, smolder with that same groundedness, that deep-rooted love for life that is absent of any kind of fear.

When I return to Pretoria from Grahamstown, I go for another morning walk. An old man pushes a cart full of dirty belongings. I can see from the corner of my eye that he is approaching me at a perpendicular angle from the left. We both stop. I look at him inquisitively, and he returns the open stare. His face is hard, stoic, unyielding. But suddenly he shifts. Something inside me breaks open, an irrepressible sense of joy and gratitude, as he raises his hand in a gesture of greeting.

Notes

Birth of the Cool

Page 3: *Thelonious Monk: Straight, No Chaser*, directed by Charlotte Zwerin. Malpreso Productions, 1988.

Page 5: James Baldwin, from "Uses of the Blues." *Playboy*, October 1964.

Fawlanioncse

Page 13: Michael Faraday, from "The Chemical History of the Candle." Fordham University, Modern History Sourcebook, 1860.

Fade to White

Page 29: from *Northern Great Lakes 2009: Michigan, Minnesota, Wisconsin.* Mobil Travel Guide.

Page 29: from "Who Is a Negro? The Inside Story of Two Million Negroes Who Passed for White," *Negro Digest* 4.12 (October 1946).

Page 30: Nuruddin Farah, from *Yesterday, Tomorrow: Voices from the Somali Diaspora.* London: Cassell, 2000.

Page 30: Jon Holtzman, from *Nuer Journeys, Nuer Lives: Sudanese Refugees in Minnesota.* Boston: Allyn and Bacon, 2000.

Page 31: Charles William Isenberg, from *Dictionary of the Amharic Language.* Ann Arbor: University of Michigan Press, 1971.

Page 32: Fanny Howe, from *The Winter Sun.* St. Paul: Graywolf, 2009.

Page 32: James Baldwin and Margaret Mead, from *A Rap on Race.* London: Corgi Books, 1971.

Page 33: Nella Larsen, from *An Intimation of Things Distant: The Collected Fiction of Nella Larsen.* New York: Anchor Books, 1992.

Page 35: Leopold Sedar Senghor, from *Prose and Poetry*, with John O. Reed and Clive Wake. London: Oxford University Press, 1965.

The Strongman and the Clown

Page 44: Victor B. Scheffer, from *The Year of the Whale*. New York: Scribner, 1969.

Page 49: Hal Whitehead, from *Voyage to the Whales*. Post Mills, VT: Chelsea Green, 1990.

Page 51: Costanzo Costantini, from *Conversations with Fellini*. New York: Harcourt Brace, 1995.

Silencing Cassandra

Page 55: Darcus Howe, from a BBC interview, August 9, 2011.

Page 55: Henry Louis Gates Jr., from "Black London." *Antioch Review* 34.3 (Spring 1976).

Page 56: P. J. Harvey, from *Let England Shake*. Vagrant Records, 2011.

Page 56: P. J. Harvey, from an interview with Dorian Lynskey for the *Guardian*, April 23, 2011.

Page 56: Anne Carson, from "The Gender of Sound," in *Glass, Irony and God*. New York: New Directions Books, 1992.

Page 60: Joseph Chaikin, from *The Presence of the Actor*. New York: Theater Communications Group, 1972.

Page 61: from *Solid Foundation: An Oral History of Reggae*, by David Katz. New York: Bloomsbury, 2003.

Page 61: Armet Francis, from Henry Louis Gates Jr., "Black London." *Antioch Review* 34.3 (Spring 1976).

Page 64: R. D. Laing, from *The Politics of Experience*. New York: Pantheon Books, 1967.

Page 66: Mike Davis, from *City of Quartz: Excavating the Future in Los Angeles*. New York: Vintage Books, 1990.

Page 66: Paula B. Johnson, David O. Sears, and John B. McConahay, from "Black Invisibility: The Press, and the Los Angeles Riot." *American Journal of Sociology* 76.4 (January 1971).

Page 68: *An Oresteia: Agamemnon by Aiskhylos; Elektra by Sophokles, Orestes by Euripedes*, trans. Anne Carson. New York: Faber and Faber, 2009.

Page 68: Les Black, from "Voices of Hate, Sounds of Hybridity: Black Music and the Complexities of Racism." *Black Music Research Journal* 20.2 (Autumn 2000).

Page 68: Klive Walker, from *Dubwise: Reasoning from the Reggae Underground*. Toronto: Insomniac Press, 2005.

Page 69: "Dread Beat an' Blood," by Poet and The Roots, produced by the dub poet Linton Kwesi Johnson, 1978.

Page 72: Patrick Barkham and Jon Henle, from "Mark Duggan: Profile of Tottenham Police Shooting Victim." *Guardian*, August 8, 2011.

Page 74: Fred Moten, from "Black Mo'nin'." In *Loss: The Politics of Mourning*, ed. David L. Eng and David Kazanjian. Berkeley: University of California Press, 2003.

Page 74: Malcolm Gladwell, from *Blink: The Power of Thinking Without Thinking*. New York: Little, Brown and Company, 2005.

Page 74: *Dictionary of Caribbean English Usage*, by Richard Allsopp and Jeannette Allsopp. Oxford: Oxford University Press, 1996.

Resolution in Bearing

Page 79: Wim Wenders, from an interview in *DoubleTake*, http://www.doubletakemagazine.org/int/html/wenders/.

Page 81: Sergei Eisenstein, from *The Film Sense*. New York: Harcourt, Brace and World, 1942.

Page 81: Oscar Wilde, as found in *The Picture of Dorian Gray; De Profundis*. New York: Modern Library, 1926.

Page 85: Ruth Watson, from "Beholding the Colonial Past in Claire Denis's Chocolat," in *Black and White in Color: African History on Screen*, ed. Vivian Bickford-Smith and Richard Mendelsohn. Athens: Ohio University Press, 2007.

Page 85: Claire Denis, from "Interview: Claire Denis on *35 Shots of Rum*," by Robert Davis. *Daily Plastic*, March 10, 2009.

Page 87: William Shakespeare, from *The Tempest*. Oxford: Oxford University Press, 1987.

Page 90: Patricia Falguieres, from *Anri Sala: When the Night Calls It a Day*. London: Walter Konig, 2004.

Page 91: *Late Spring*, directed by Yasurjiro Ozu. Shochiku Films Ltd. 1949.

Page 93: Michael Atkinson, from "Late Spring: Home with Ozu," http://www.criterion.com/current/posts/421-late-spring-home-with-ozu

Page 95: Michelle Alexander, from Dick Price, "More Black Men Now in Prison System Than Enslaved in 1850." *LA Progressive*, March 2011.

Page 95: *Songs from the Capeman*, by Paul Simon. Warner Brothers, 1997.

Page 96: Adrian Piper, from *Out of Order, Out of Sight: Selected Writings in Meta-Art, Volume One, 1968–1992*. Cambridge, MA: MIT Press, 1996.

Cicatrization

Page 107: Angela Fisher, from *Africa Adorned*. New York: Harry N. Abrams, 1984.

Page 109: Mark Stevens, from "Human Nature." *New York Magazine*, May 2005.

Page 109: Coco Fusco, from *English Is Broken Here: Notes on Cultural Fusion in the Americas*. New York: New City Press, 1995.

Page 110: Margaret Courtney-Clarke, from *African Canvas*. New York: Rizzoli, 1990.

Page 110: Susan Sontag, from *Regarding the Pain of Others*. New York: Picador, 2003.

Page 111: Countee Cullen, from "Heritage," in *Color*. New York: Harper and Brothers, 1925.

Page 118: Eula Biss, from *Notes from No Man's Land*. St. Paul: Graywolf, 2009.

Page 124: Christine Redfern, from *Who Is Ana Mendieta?* New York: The Feminist Press, 2011.

Acknowledgments and Permissions

Thank you to Lorraine Sabatini for the showers upon showers upon showers of love. Thank you to Lester Sloan for cutting away the branches on this path of ours so that I could so easily follow. I am unthinkably lucky to have artists for parents. Thank you, Argusta Sloan, for telling me what to do when the train comes. Thank you to Lisa Sloan, for explaining Kwame Kilpatrick and for your gracious sisterhood. Thank you, Jeremy and LaShawn Mulligan, for letting me be your aunt even when it's you who teach me so much about writing, strength, and how to smile at cameras. Thanks to Juliette McGrew for swinging your purse in my defense, bringing me poets, and teaching me to keep my heart open always. Thank you, Rebecca Iosca, for hours of epiphany and messy days that always yield a bigger picture. Thank you, Arianne Zwartjes, for this intrepid friendship, for looking out the door at night when I get scared. Thank you, Keevil, for your accidental Buddhism, your straight talk and equilibrium. Thank you, Beth Alvarado, for making all of this possible, for your thoughtful letters of response to every essay I've ever written, and for a mentorship that always draws my attention to possibility.

Thank you, Sarah Donnelly, for the architecture of your dreaming. Thank you to Logan Byers, for being there with me to witness the man who wove on his rollerblades like a ballerina through oncoming traffic. Thank you, Julie Baron, for knowing always when to swoop, pointing out other owls and realigning my pigeon pose. Thank you to Tucson Yoga, Frank Jude Boccio, and our sangha for the gift of presence. Thank you, Lisa O'Neill, Debbie Weingarten, Maria Moore, Desiree Washington, and Julie Lauterbach-Colby, for spice racks and steam. Thank you to Kofi Owusu, Greg Hewett, and William North for guiding me through the project that led me to write this book. Thank you to Les Klein for teaching me that analysis can be a form of compassion. Thank you to the *Disquiet* Summer Workshop in Portugal and to my Lisbon friends for introducing me to a world of literature that is an adventure of sweet coincidence. Thank you to my teachers and wonderful MFA workshop at the University of Arizona for laughter and brilliance and piggybacking.

Thank you to my godmother, Katherine A. Smith, and my uncle, Paul Sabatini, for being ferociously intelligent and for telling stories over the dinner table. Thank you to Becky Sabatini for keeping the dream of Italy alive. Thank you to my cousin Benjamin for admitting that I won at pool. Thank you to Angelina Burnett for being the multimedia projectionist of my subconscious mind. Thank you, everyone in my family, for love. Thank you, all my friends, for friendship and wisdom, especially those of you who helped dream this book into being: Susannah Masur, Holly Hill, Jill Golden, Radhika Garland, Heather Turner, Ruth Curry, Nishta Mehra, Amanda Sapir, Daisy Pitkin, Vievee Francis, and Barbara Cully. Thank you, Baldwin, for going without so many walks and sleeping with your ears out like wings.

Thank you to Fanny Howe for selecting an earlier version of this book as a finalist in the 2011 *1913* First Book Contest. Thank you Simmons Buntin and Joshua Foster for giving me a chance on *Terrain.org.* Thank you to the editors of *Identity Theory* for publishing "Birth of the Cool" (August 2009) and to the editors of *Writing as Revision* for anthologizing it (Third Edition, 2010). Thank you to *Michigan Quarterly Review* for publishing "Fawlanionese" (49.3, Summer 2010). Thank you to *Ninth Letter* for publishing "Fade to White" (8.1, Spring/Summer 2011). Thank you to *Southern Review* for publishing "The Strongman and the Clown" (Winter, 2013). Thank you to my students for keeping my mind sharp and teaching me "How to Love"—literally and the version by Lil Wayne. Thank you Jonathan Kirsch for your guidance. Thank you to David Coen for copyediting these sentences. Thank you to the University of Iowa Press, especially Carl Klaus, Charlotte Wright, Allison Means, Karen Copp, and Catherine Cocks, and the wonderful Joseph Parsons, who found me on my birthday.

sightline books
The Iowa Series in Literary Nonfiction